MASTER AIRMAN

For the boys and girls of Pathfinder Group.

Master Airman

A Biography of
Air Vice-Marshal
Donald Bennett, CB., CBE., DSO.

Alan Bramson

Airlife
ENGLAND

By the same author

BE A BETTER PILOT
MAKE BETTER LANDINGS
THE BOOK OF FLIGHT TESTS
PRINCIPLES OF FLIGHT (Audio-visual)

As co-author

THE TIGER MOTH STORY
CAPTAINS AND KINGS
A GUIDE TO AIRCRAFT OWNERSHIP
RADIO NAVIGATION FOR PILOTS
FLYING THE VOR
FLIGHT BRIEFING FOR MICROLIGHT PILOTS
FLIGHT BRIEFING FOR PILOTS
    Vol.1 An Introductory Manual of Flying Training
    Vol.2 An advanced Manual of Flying Training
    Vol.3 Radio Aids to Air Navigation
    Vol.4 Ground Instruction
    Vol.5 Flight Emergency Procedures
    Vol.6 Examination Questions and Answers
    Vol.7 The IMC Rating
    Vol.8 The Instrument Rating

ISBN 0 906393 45 0

First published 1985
by Airlife Publishing Ltd.

Printed in England by Livesey Ltd., Shrewsbury.

Airlife Publishing Ltd.

7 St. John's Hill, Shrewsbury, England.

Contents

Acknowledgements

When writing a book of this kind the author is entirely dependent upon sources of information. Official and other records are, of course, valuable but they cannot entirely replace the all-important face-to-face interview. Without such interviews even the best of writers is unable to paint a true picture of his subject. Faced with unfilled gaps in his knowledge the only alternatives are conjecture, the inspired guess or simply words born of the writer's own imagination. Such expedients are bound to detract from the accuracy of a biography and I am therefore very grateful to the many important and outstanding people who readily agreed to meet me when it became known that a long overdue biography of Don Bennett was to be written.

It would be impossible to list the names of all willing helpers but I wish to thank Don and Ly Bennett who spent so much time with me and who endured my lengthy and sometimes persistent questioning. Marshal of the Royal Air Force Sir Arthur Harris devoted best part of a day to me and I am particularly sad that the great man did not live to see this book — he was very proud of his prodigy, Don Bennett. I am particularly grateful to Lady Harris for agreeing to that meeting.

In the course of preparing this book I have enjoyed the enthusiastic support of Group Captain 'Hamish' Mahaddie, Pathfinder's legendary Inspector of Training who worked so closely with Bennett during the war. Without the help of Air Marshal Sir Ivor Broom, Air Vice-Marshal Sidney Bufton, Group Captain Leonard Cheshire VC, Group Captain Geoffrey Womersley, Alex Thorn, Captain Gordon Store and Mrs. Dorothy Grey it would not have been possible for me to record some of the factual detail that is so essential in a book of this kind. I would like to thank Mr. Ian C. Graham, Senior Librarian at the Royal Signals and Radar Establishment for providing valuable references relating to the various wartime radio aids.

Because of the remarkable nature of the man and his widely differing accomplishments, the writing of *Master Airman, the Biography of Air Vice-Marshal Donald Bennett.* has been a massive if enjoyable task. Fortunately I have enjoyed the help and constructive advice of my wife Miriam. Finally I should like to thank Vivienne Orr for so beautifully typing the manuscript.

Author's Foreword

When a man becomes a legend in his own lifetime it is usually the case that only his closest friends and associates really get to know him. To the great majority of people rumour, myth and half-truth portray an often distorted picture of the individual. With time these widely held beliefs gather all manner of embroidery so that popular impression bears little relationship to the famous personality in question.

On learning that I had been invited to write a biography of Air Vice-Marshal Donald Bennett several aquaintances, some of them claiming first-hand knowledge of the man, said " — you will find him impossible to get on with — a fire eater — impatient, demanding and only intent on having his own way".

Prior to starting this book I had only met Don Bennett on a few, brief occasions and the picture I had been given seemed at variance with what I had observed. Now, having spent many hours asking countless questions, some of them of a personal and perhaps accusing nature, I can tell readers of this book that Don Bennett is not the least as portrayed by those claiming first-hand knowledge of the great man. True he has his obsessions. True he is a perfectionist (a characteristic guaranteed to damn him in the eyes of the lazy). Equally true, during the war, when the balance between instant defeat and the survival of Britain could have been influenced by a puff of wind in either direction, Don Bennett would not suffer fools gladly. But surely that was a good thing for Britain because, if ever the phrase had any meaning, he was the right man at the right time.

It has been an absorbing and fascinating task writing *Master Airman, the Biography of Air Vice-Marshal Donald Bennett.* I have met some of the greatest names in wartime Bomber Command and other walks of life. And I have come to understand and admire Don Bennett.

A.E.B.
London 1985

Chapter 1
Boyhood Days

Inside that tube of a Lancaster fuselage seven highly trained aircrew go about their various tasks. The pilot flies on instruments while his flight engineer constantly monitors the engine readouts, ready to detect a malfunction. Behind them the radio operator wills his ears to recognise the dots and dashes of a morse signal that may bring good or bad news.

In a little office, cut off from the real world, the navigator concentrates on the latest advanced radio aids as they twitch and blink their information on little green cathode ray tubes. On his table are the charts that have got them to the target area — now they must find the aiming point.

Up front, lying prone in the very nose of the big, four-engined aircraft, is the bomb aimer, squinting through his sophisticated bomb sight, release button poised to deliver ten tons of high explosive aimed at knocking a few noughts off Hitler's so called "1000 year Reich". Above him, in a power-operated turret is the front gunner. Along with two colleagues, one located in a midupper turret and another with four guns in the tail he is responsible for discouraging German night fighter pilots with ambitions to gain an Iron Cross.

Inside, all activity and even the bare bones of the aircraft, are saturated by the throaty roar of four Rolls-Royce Merlin engines. A sound like the bowing of a thousand string bass players, it is music to the ears of Lancaster crews and a message of fear to those waiting for the onslaught below.

Outside the darkness is broken by the flash of anti-aircraft guns, bursting shells and stabbing searchlights which reveal cloud cover above and a patchwork of broken stratus below. A flaming Lancaster spins its way almost leisurely to the ground, victim of an enemy night fighter or one of the German radar-controlled guns — will they ever know which? Whatever the cause someone will not return for bacon and eggs tonight or perhaps ever again.

Down on the ground red target indicators are joined by cascades of green which burst about half a mile to the right. The radio comes into life "Cancel the red, bomb the green — cancel the red, bomb the green" — the voice of the Master Bomber, boss man and controller of the raid. Now all hell is let loose. Aircraft of the main bomber force stream in to drop their loads and at intervals 'backers-up' re-mark the aiming point with coloured target indicators. For an outsider it is a picture of utter confusion but to the trained eyes and ears of the Master Bomber everything is going according to plan.

Three years previously not one bomb in fifty found its way to within three miles of the target. Now things are very different because the Pathfinder Force has perfected its target finding talents to a fine art, it's youthful leader continually striving for new techniques, higher levels of skill and standards of professionalism that would have been considered unattainable when the RAF first started to attack the mighty German war machine with obsolete aircraft, archaic methods and puny bombs. Yes indeed, for very good reason the name Don Bennett is well known to the Germans.

Men of similar rank and responsibility in the RAF are, in the main, twenty or more years older than Bennett yet his technical knowledge, flying skill and experience is probably unequalled in any air force on either side of the conflict. What forces of circumstance and family upbringing create the likes of Bennett, a man who became an aviation legend before he was thirty and a name calculated to command the respect of the great German Wehrmacht?

*   *   *   *

In the mid-nineteenth century a citizen named Bennett emigrated from Northern Ireland to Australia. There he met and married a Miss Makepeace and a son, George Thomas was later born in Ipswich, Queensland.

On the other side of the world, in fact months away in terms of contemporary boat travel, one Doctor T. P. Lucas was embroiled in a struggle for recognition with that ultra conservative and august body, the British Medical Association. He claimed a degree of success in the treatment of cancer through the use of

Pau Pau fruit; the BMA would have none of it. Such was the hostility generated by his exchanges with the British medical establishment that when his wife died Dr. Lucas upped sticks and set course for Australia, taking with him his daughter, Celia Juliana. There the London-born girl met George Thomas Bennett, they married and it was not long before things were booming on the Bennett home front. George Thomas had a talent for raising cattle on the grand scale and while business grew and prospered the young couple began to produce a family of outstanding brillance.

Clyde Kinsey Bennett was born at the turn of the century. He became a successful barrister. Aubrey George followed eighteen months later and he was destined to be a talented eye specialist. Six-and-a-half years were to pass before Arnold Lucas Bennett arrived. He became one of the most distinguished QCs in Queensland.

On 14 September 1910 Donald Clifford Tyndall arrived, the fourth of the Bennett boys. At this time the family were residing in Toowoomba, Southern Queensland, in those days a country town with dust roads and few facilities. Even the main high street was unsurfaced and it was much as one might imagine a Mid West town made famous by the cowboy films. In 1920 between thirty and forty thousand people lived in Toowoomba, situated at the top of the Great Divide, seventy miles west of Brisbane the capital of Queensland. By 1928 they were beginning to surface the roads.

Life at home for the four Bennett brothers was a happy one based on self-discipline, the older boys being expected to set an example to their juniors. It worked well, although the oldest boy could come down hard when the others stepped out of line. When the boys went to school in a pony and trap driven by Clyde, big brother was very much captain of the ship. Relationship between parents and children was warm; there were few taboos at home but on no account were the boys allowed to bring dogs into the house.

Father's cattle station was at a place called Kanimbla on the Condamine river, 180 square miles of it supporting 2000 Herefords. Today such an area would feed 10,000 head of cattle but so much has changed — in those days cattle grazers regarded sheep farming as something only for old men. The great depression hit Australia before other countries but the Bennett family lived comfortably enough. They were among the first in that part of rural Queensland to own motor cars. At the age of only four or perhaps five the young Don Bennett would steer a model T Ford while sitting on his father's knee. Certainly by the time he was eleven Don was allowed to drive the family Overland within the estate and at an early age all the boys had their own cars. These they were required to maintain scrupulously although father raised no objection when the boys indulged in a little motor racing.

Although the Great War that embroiled Europe in 1914 was being waged some twelve thousand miles away Australian servicemen were involved in all three branches of the armed forces. The vast distance that separated Australians from the conflict did nothing to diminish their concern or their interest in the bloody events being enacted in the fields and cities of Belgium and France. Don Bennett was only four years old when World War I started but by 1917 Clyde, his oldest brother, could stand aside no longer. He enlisted in the Australian Flying Corps only to be rejected because he was under age.

Like most brothers the Bennett boys played the usual 'hunter and hunted' games and it was during one of these games that the young Donald exhibited a side to his character that was to see him through the most daunting of situations. Cornered by the other three boys and in a position where most lads would have conceded defeat, the older boys were astonished to see 'little brother' leap 25 feet from a tree into some lantana bushes from whence he emerged unmarked and unshaken. From that moment on was born the family party trick which became know as the 'Lantana Jump'.

A less spectacular but nevertheless convincing demonstration of courage occurred when Don Bennett was twelve. The older boys left him to control a number of cows lined up against a fence while they walked to a nearby village. The sun went down, the stillness of a dark Australian night was violated by the howl of wild dogs and to the little boy father's cattle, so friendly before dark, now assumed threatening proportions. He began to lose his nerve when what appeared to be a large bull walked purposefully towards him. The 'bull' turned out to be his brothers.

Don Bennett was particularly attached to his brother Aubrey. Even as a boy his humanity, unusual in one so young, influenced the others. On a number of occasions the older boy was to offer the baby of the family sound advice and encouragement although there was one episode involving another of the brothers, where the roles of supporter and supported were reversed. Donald and Arnold who was two years his senior had gone exploring up the

Lamington Plateau. They went on and on through narrow tracks, the lads gradually becoming exhausted. Soon they were having to stop at fifty yard intervals. It became dark and to add to their troubles the dog, driven frantic by a tick, took off in a state of near madness and was probably devoured by the dingos. At that stage Arnold said he was unable to go any further but the younger lad went on alone, found the plateau, dumped his pack then went back and fetched his brother. For the first time in his life little brother had been able to prove himself, something he was to demonstrate on countless occasions in the years ahead.

The boys went to a typically British type of prep school which was run by an Englishman named Gill. Then father moved house to Brisbane and the three older boys were given private schooling. However, it rapidly became clear that the young Donald was not in the same academic mould as the others and Bennett senior, no doubt wary of throwing away hard-earned money on a son who was unwilling to work at what others thought necessary (but he considered dull) sent his youngest offspring to Brisbane Grammar School. Not that young Donald was a dunce, far from it, he managed to top his physics class and do well in chemistry. His maths was quiet good also but history, geography and languages were a closed book. Sixty years later Don Bennett makes light of his school record. In mock anguish he will say "I didn't matriculate — uneducated — disgrace of the family".

A particularly critical school report finally decided Bennett senior that there was nothing to be gained by forcing education down the throat of his youngest and it was decided that Don would work in the property office he had opened in town. Like so many talented people Don Bennett was unable to devote time and energy to what, in his eyes, was uninteresting. But give these same people an opportunity of working in an environment of their own choosing and nothing can stand in their way while perfection is being achieved. So it was with Don Bennett, although at this stage of his life it is doubtful if he had the slightest notion that aviation would be his passport to fame and achievement. From an early age Don had been a practical lad, building canoes with his brothers, re-building cars and the like. Guiding passion among the Bennett boys was surfing but then they lived in the right part of the world for that; for sheer power Pacific rollers are unmatched anywhere in Europe and after a time surf boards were considered 'cissy'. The boys came over the top of these giant waves of unbelievable power, bodies stiff and ready to drop vertically down the other side before planing away. To them surfing with boards was *passé*.

It was brother Aubrey who first floated the idea that father's cattle station could do with a little diversification of interest. Breeding for beef was all very well but why not start a dairy division? So without asking Bennett senior the brothers rounded up thirty or more good looking heifers and brought them into the home paddock. Now the cattle on an Australian beef-producing station are not to be confused with the Jerseys and Herefords on the tranquil English farming scene. These Australian heifers were wild in the real meaning of the word. And they did not take kindly to being milked. The station manager viewed these activities with some dismay and tried hard to discourage the brothers but they assured the older and wiser man that father would approve when he learned of the enterprise. The plan was to drive a few cows into the branding crush (stockade), tie them up and start milking.

One of the heifers struggled so violently that the poor beast broke a leg. This was the last straw for the station manager; he jumped onto a horse and rode thirty miles to the nearest telegraph office, sent a message to Bennett senior and that was the end of dairy farming.

In the main they were happy days on the cattle station. By a strange coincidence some sixty years after these events Don Bennett and his wife took a flat in the Condamine district of Monte Carlo. The river running through his father's cattle station is called the Condamine. To young Donald in particular, raising great herds of cattle was an attractive occupation. The trouble was he liked it so much that at the tender age of seventeen he had fears of dissolving into the countryside. True enough, the life appealed and unlike the older brothers there was no doctor or lawyer within, awaiting the cultivation of university and good teaching. He may be the non-academic of the family but there was a lot more inside the most junior member of the family than following in father's footsteps.

There was a vague idea that he rather liked aeroplanes, nothing very definite the way some girls want to be nurses and many boys like cars, but it was there nevertheless. When the interest occurred is difficult to pinpoint, but around 1913 an American pilot visited Toowoomba in one of the stick-and-wire flying machines of the day. Aubrey grabbed brothers Arnold and Donald by the hand and they ran across the fields to watch. Arnold would have been five years old at the time and Don was two years younger. Who can say what passes through the minds of such children on seeing an aeroplane for the first time, but as previously mentioned Arnold became an outstanding QC and having been knighted in 1975 decided to take up flying two years later. On 12 November 1978, his 70th birthday, three generations of his family forgathered at the Coolangatta Aero Club where he gave joyrides to some of his five daughters, three sons and nineteen grandchildren. Lady Bennett had been his first passenger after gaining a Private Pilot Licence.

With Donald Bennett the infection with aviation was rather different. When he was fifteen a friend by name of G. N. Wickner (cousin of Edgar Percival, the famous aircraft designer and manufacturer) bought an old Maurice Farman. It was in a packing case and Don Bennett took an active part in assembling and rigging the old biplane with its profusion of piano wire bracing and little metal fittings. The boys must have done a good job because it flew well until the 'qualified' pilot entrusted with the controls clipped the top of a barbed wire fence during take-off, turned the Maurice Farman onto its back and wrecked it beyond economical repair. A number of events gave stimulus to Don's latent interest in aircraft. There was the arrival of Bert Hinkler after his flight from England to Australia, the moment when an exhausted Amy Johnson, first woman to fly solo from England to Australia, turned over while landing in a corn field and the arrival of Charles Kingsford-Smith at the end of his epic Pacific flight. Having regard to the lack of instruments and navigation aids at the time Don Bennett regards this as one of the greatest flights in the history of aviation.

Possibly the most important single factor which led Don Bennett into aviation was the influence of favourite brother Aubrey, himself very airminded although he did not become a pilot. At one stage of his career Aubrey was appointed Resident Medical Officer of an Outback area which Don Bennett would describe as "fifteen hundred miles of nothing". Visits to his emergency patients at the cattle stations were made in an old DH 9A flown by the legendary Lester Brain who was the first pilot to be employed by Qantas, the first flying instructor in Brisbane and, in the eyes of young Donald, an out-and-out glamour boy. The Bennett family was not without its aviation connections. Apart from Aubrey visiting the sick by air (and anticipating the Australian Flying Doctor by many years) father was friendly with the famous Hudson Fysh who in the mid 1920s was managing director of Qantas. However, in that period aviation had more than its share of accidents throughout the world and

Australia was no exception. So when at the age of seventeen Donald Bennett let it be known that he wanted to join the Royal Australian Air Force the disclosure dropped like a bomb and provoked little enthusiasm from his parents. Mother tried to discourage her youngest son on two counts; the accident records clearly indicated that flying was dangerous. And in those days being a pilot was not regarded as a profession because it did not entail gaining a university degree. It was, in her eyes, a dangerous and thoroughly low-brow activity. Father held similar views but nevertheless adopted a generous position. He would say "It's your life — you do what you want".

Looking back on this period of Don Bennett's life it would be fair to say that both parents were very tolerant. Aviation was relatively primitive at the time and the thought of her youngest son becoming a pilot was particularly hard for Celia Bennett. Her father had been a doctor and so was her second son. Two of the boys were making careers in the law and not unnaturally she wanted her fourth child to become a doctor. But Donald Bennett had made up his mind to join the RAAF and he enjoyed the support of brother Aubrey, by now an air passenger of some experience and in a good position to know at first hand that flying need not be dangerous if it is treated with respect and so long as pilots adopt professional attitudes. "Every activity has its dangers" he would tell his parents, "Are you going to stand in the way of Don doing most other things?"

The youngest age for enrolment in the RAAF was 18 and Don Bennett spent the following year gaining useful legal experience drawing up agreements in the family property office. There had always been a latent interest in matters mechanical and to fill in time before going into the RAAF he joined as a night student at Queensland University. There he studied engineering. But when time came to sit the entrance examination and pass the interview before acceptance into the Service the young Don Bennett was to experience his first real conflict with officialdom and bureaucracy, a conflict that was to continue over many, many years and even to the present day.

Chapter 2
The Fledgling

A Supermarine Southampton flying boat of the Royal Australian Air Force flew up from Point Cooke, Victoria to Brisbane. In it was the interviewing board headed by Group Captain Gobble, an Englishman serving with the RAAF and Squadron Leader Browning. It was the practice in those days to allocate places on a regional basis, so many from the Melbourne area, so many from Sydney etc. Of the 1500 young men who applied for pilot training only fifteen were selected and four of these were transfers from the Duntroon Military College which was feeling the effects of the Depression and glad to be ridding itself of a few cadets. More than three hundred aspiring pilots had applied from the Queensland area and, notwithstanding the fact that he had failed to matriculate, Don Bennett came top in the examination and interview. They gave him a rail warrant and joining instructions; he seemed poised on the edge of a new life.

A week before he was due to join the RAAF a telegram arrived. It said "Your appointment to the Royal Australian Air Force cancelled". A not very illuminating exchange of telegrams culminated in a cryptic if polite reply which said "Regret you have been rejected on medical grounds". It was an irate Don Bennett who burst in on his doctor clutching the offending telegram. "Is this your doing?" he enquired accusingly. Of course government departments, civil and military, are run almost entirely on forms and to the question asking if Don had retained or lost his tonsils the family doctor had merely stated the truth. There could be no other medical reason for his rejection by the RAAF — it had to be tonsils. "Take them out now" insisted Don Bennett and with no more than a local anaesthetic the deed was done in the doctor's surgery. "Tonsils removed" said Bennett's telegram to the RAAF at Melbourne. "You are rejected" came the reply.

At that stage most teenagers would have given up the unequal fight with bureaucracy but the Bennett boy, youngest of his tribe, had other ideas. With money borrowed from his parents he made the 1500 mile rail journey to Melbourne, walked into the Air Board offices at 8.30 the following morning and there confronted Group Captain Gobble. A direct conversation followed in the course of which the Group Captain became more and more impressed with the tenacity of young Don, so much so that he agreed to accept him on the next course. It later transpired that the nephew of a politician had been rejected by the RAAF. Uncle had threatened trouble, the Air Board had weakened so one cadet had to be dropped to make room. Who better than the lad from Toowoomba? That such a thing could happen in Australia came as a shock to Don Bennett but the lesson was learned and it did him good.

The delay was probably a good thing for Don Bennett. Two courses before his, eleven out of fifteen cadets had been killed while learning to fly, mainly as a result of engine failures. Had he joined the Royal Australian Air Force on the original date he would have found morale at Point Cooke in poor shape and a station in the throes of changing aircraft. As it was, he went home for six months while they cleaned up the mess and got themselves back to normal.

Point Cooke is on the western shore of Port Phillip. In those days it was a mixed land and marine air station. Slipways were provided for two Supermarine Southampton flying boats and five Seagull amphibians. The airfield suffered from lack of drainage. There were, of course, no runways in 1929 and following heavy rain the field would dissolve into a patchwork of mud and ruts which later baked rock hard in the Australian sun. Like many military airfields the world over, Point Cooke was designed to provide the maximum of inconvenience to all on the station. Hangars and workshops were on the side of the airfield adjacent to the sea while the parade ground and barracks were more than a mile away on the other side. No doubt those responsible for planning the installation would remind their critics of the exercise they had provided for all who served. In real terms Point Cooke was an example of planning without intelligent thought; to those responsible time and motion studies were a closed book.

It is also part of the ritual in most services for the cadets to hold their own unofficial initiation ceremony. Usually they are harmless enough affairs, bordering on the moronic. At Point

Cooke the initiation was over-wild and potentially dangerous. Horseplay involved everything from sitting blindfold, bare-behind on a block of ice to risk of being permanently maimed by a red hot poker. It transcended the point of reason and ceased to be fun. Eventually the risk of injuring valuable potential pilots caused the authorities to place restrictions on the scope of these initiation ceremonies but from all accounts they were even more dangerous than the somewhat hazardous flying training of the day.

The first week at Point Cooke was intended to kill off all but the most determined. Drill was intensive, cadets made and remade their beds with precision, polished the floors until to walk on them was to risk slipping and breaking a leg, and carried out the usual mindless and unproductive 'bull' which probably reached its highest levels of stupidity in the American flying schools during the Second World War.

The cadets lived in the Officers' Mess. They wore the navy uniform of the RAAF with white flashes to denote their cadet status. Every morning at 7 am would see them lined up outside their rooms. They would shave, wash, have breakfast and report on parade at 8 am. The cadets then joined the rest of the station and marched a mile to the hangars where flying training would start for the morning. There was another mile-long march back to the mess for lunch followed by a return march for lectures. Ground training with the RAAF was in those days more comprehensive than that provided for Royal Air Force cadet pilots in Britain. The Australian on a wings course was shown how to use a lathe, principles of flight were taught in considerable depth and students were required to understand aerial photography. However, the standard of navigation training was poor.

By the time Don Bennett was at Point Cooke the Avro 504K trainers were mostly replaced by de Havilland Cirrus Moths. These had no airspeed indicators other than a flat plate mounted on a spring with a pointer reading MPH, a crude but effective gadget located on the forward interplane strut between the left wings. Wartime pilots in Britain will remember seeing these airspeed indicators which supplemented the ASI mounted on the instrument panel of Tiger Moths. Some of the Cirrus Moths carried 8 lb practice bombs and these were aimed against a floating target in Port Phillip.

Flight Commander for *ab initio* training was F/Lt. Jerry Walters. Don Bennett's instructor, Sergeant Preston, was no ball of fire, but he was sound and painstaking and he knocked out of the young Bennett any element of snobbery that might have been lurking under the surface. Many of his fellow cadets may have had commissioned instructors. But his sergeant made him top of the course and that lesson remained with him in later life.

Ronald Ramsey Rae was a fellow cadet with Don Bennett at Point Cooke. These were days before he could fly properly and the prized qualifying wings were anything but a foregone conclusion, yet Bennett set about writing a training manual on navigation. Were these the seeds of his deep interest in the subject which later made him one of the world's leading experts on air navigation? Rae remembers the young Donald as being serious minded and regarded by the other cadets as rather puritanical because he neither smoked nor drank (something he does not do to this day).

At Point Cooke the cadets were given sixty hours elementary instruction in the Moths followed by another 60 in the mammouth Westland Wapiti, a towering biplane with a big propeller which rotated so slowly you could actually see it going round.

One of the favourite cross-country flights was to a place in the next state called Deniliquin, New South Wales. The route was over 200 miles of almost featureless terrain, terminating in a landing on five miles of lawn-standard grass. Another highlight of the course was an aerial survey. Cadets filled the cameras, flew the aircraft, took the pictures, developed the film, printed it and then pasted down a mosaic. In later years, during World War 2, Don Bennett had good reason to value the experience, particularly when the group photographic section tried to blind him with science on one or two occasions. It was Bennett who demanded stereo photographs during the war and these were of enormous value when the V1 sites first came to light.

The Wapiti was used for realistic bombing practice, far more convincing than the Moths and their little 8 lb bombs. World War I surplus 112 lb bombs were dropped in the bay and almost invariably several sharks would be killed during these exercises. The Wapiti was very reliable and forced landings due to engine failure were unknown.

So with the end of the course in sight and 120 hours in his log book Don Bennett took the final flying test and sat the exams. He came top in flying and second in ground school. Of the original 15 cadets eleven had passed. His white flashes were replaced by the thin sleeve band of a Pilot Officer and a service career seemed assured until the newly qualified pilots were summoned to a special meeting, there to receive the bad news. The RAAF was short of money, they were told. Well this came as no surprise because in 1929 the Great Depression which afflicted most of the industrial world was having its effect. But what followed burst like a bomb in the room. Then and there these bright and talented young men who had given of their best in the demanding course at Point Cooke were told "You can either get out — or get out" the alternatives being to leave the service or go to Britain and be seconded to the RAF. Half the course refused to leave Australia and sail for England; Bennett and four others readily agreed although almost immediately the new RAAF/RAF deal became known as 'the Slave Market'.

Don Bennett's mother was delighted with the news and lost no time in impressing on her youngest son how lucky he was to be visiting the old country. But then Celia Bennett was more English than the English, something that often happens to folk from the UK who live abroad. Not a trace of Australian accent was ever allowed among the Bennett boys and if any one of them dared to lapse into the faintest suggestion of 'down-under' talk mother would say "Stop speaking like an American".

Looking back on the sequence of events that placed Bennett on loan to the RAF in England it is interesting to contemplate what might have been but for the Australian Depression. No doubt Pilot Officer Bennett would have remained with the RAAF, moving up the promotion ladder, partly on seniority, partly on merit. But the move to England opened up all manner of opportunities that could not have presented themselves in his native Australia. In his own country he would have been just another professional airman. The posting to England was to confront him with situations of the most challenging nature. But his character thrived on challenge — the bigger the better.

Chapter 3
An Australian in the RAF

The *Narkunda,* a P & O ship in the old, pre-war tradition, used to plough its way back and forth between England and Australia. These days we think in terms of spending hours in a large aircraft or, at the most, little more than a day. The sea journey was, of course, totally different — weeks of space, grace and good food instead of having to eat from a little partitioned tray and the indignity of queuing for one of the few plumbing facilities provided for perhaps 400 or more passengers in a modern jet.

Following his agreement to place himself on loan to the Royal Air Force, Pilot Officer D.C.T. Bennett sailed on the *Narkunda* travelling first class *via* Ceylon, Bombay, Aden, the Suez Canal, Malta and Gibraltar. The trip presented Don Bennett with his first opportunity of meeting the 'Pommies' *en masse;* at Bombay they took on board a number of Indian Army officers and their families. The men, he thought, were not a bad crowd but the women he describes as "loud-mouthed, over-bearing, pompous and stupid".

RAF station Uxbridge was a new experience for Bennett. Back home he rarely met anyone above the rank of Squadron Leader (Major, in Army terms). At Uxbridge 'scrambled egg' was everywhere, that official-looking gold braid on the officers' caps, a single row for Group Captains (Colonels), two lots when the officer was an Air Commodore or even more senior. He was surrounded by top brass and yet, being a Royal Air Force station, the atmosphere was not daunting although they dressed for dinner every night.

The Australians were allowed to wear their own navy uniforms, but it had been agreed under the terms of the attachment that those who wished could buy RAF uniforms. Some of his Australian colleagues thought that Bennett should have worn his Australian navy. So he did, on occasions, as a reminder that he was on loan to the RAF, but he was not prepared to 'rub their noses in it' by only wearing his navy uniform.

The next course to move from Australia to England included ex-colleague Ronald Ramsay Rae. He recalls that Don Bennett was at the docks to meet the ship, show the new arrivals around London and advise them about dealing with the 'Pommies'. It was an act of kindness representing another side to the young man's complex character.

First introduction to the air over Britain was in a World War I Bristol Fighter at RAF Sealand near Chester. The idea was for the RAF to assess standards of training and flying skill of their Australian guests. The flying itself was no problem but after the sparse countryside of Australia, with its few but unmistakable ground features, map reading in highly developed England proved surprisingly difficult. There were, of course, no radio aids and navigation in small aircraft relied heavily on selecting the right features on the map and then finding them on the ground.

By the time Don Bennett got to fly the Bristols these splendid old two-seat fighters were long since obsolete but they did enable the RAF to check pilots in an aircraft not far removed in performance from current service equipment. A week at Sealand was followed by posting to No. 29 Squadron, North Weald in Essex there to fly a contemporary fighter, the Armstrong Whitworth Siskin. Don Bennett came to regard these little biplanes as among the worst aircraft ever to be designed, a view that was apparently shared by his squadron commander, an Irishman named Paddy O'Neal who would go to great lengths and adopt the most ingenious ploys while avoiding the Siskin. It was unstable in pitch, roll and yaw. One of the flight commanders was another Irishman called Duke. Both sons of the Emerald Isle were wise men but they could never agree although, being Irish, they were able to teach Bennett a lot about the English.

Don Bennett's first experience of night flying was in the twitchy little Siskin. The landing area at North Weald was less than 1000 yards long and 'runway lighting' consisted of three paraffin flares. Considering the reliability, or rather the lack of reliability of fighter engines in those days, it is perhaps hard to credit that Siskin pilots were allowed to fly over London at night. Bennett and his colleagues tried their hand at low level map reading over the streets of London and found it almost impossible to distinguish one feature from another with any degree of certainty. The experience stayed with him during the war years to come and so fixed his opinions on low level flying at night over built-up areas that he would have none of it. When the need arose for low level target marking, it was another distinguished RAF bomber pilot who proved that it could be done, provided circumstances were ideal for the technique. Having been brought up by an English mother it was not hard for Don Bennett to melt into the English scenery. There was not the least suggestion of an Australian accent (although brother Arnold who was later knighted and who got himself a pilot's licence at the age of 70 was an unmistakable 'strine'). Looking back on life for an Australian in Britain of the early 1930s Bennett will tell you that, in general, the English thought the Aussies were coarse, primitive and uneducated (which he freely admits was true of the times) while the Australians thought the English were 'a bunch of softies'. There was a degree of mutual disrespect although through the powerful, common interest of service flying they got on well enough.

During his year on Siskins at North Weald Don Bennett rapidly recognised that being in Britain represented a wonderful opportunity for gaining aviation knowledge. While his colleagues were happy enough to do their jobs, then lead the good life of a peace-time RAF officer, he was hell bent on volunteering for every course the RAF could offer. It was not all that easy to be accepted on these courses; the RAF was no different to the Army and Navy; money had to be spent in pennies because the politicians were watching developments in Hitler's Germany with non-seeing eyes. Nevertheless he 'invited' himself on to a parachute course. They sent you to RAF Henlow where the art of parachute packing was taught. Next came instruction on how to land without breaking a leg (or even worse) followed by a live drop.

For parachute dropping the RAF used obsolete Vickers Vimy bombers, giant twin-engine biplanes held rigid by an array of struts and bracing wires. On each lower wing adjacent to the outer interplane struts was a small platform. Two trainee parachutists stood, one on each wing, feet on the platforms, facing backwards with the arms clasped around the interplane strut. The pilot took off, climbed to a safe height then gave a signal whereupon the two trainees, each wearing an additional parachute in case the main canopy failed to open, carefully shuffled around to the back of his strut. He was now facing forward clasping the strut before him. The aircraft would have been flying at around 60 mph and the pilot was supposed to know when his trainees should 'hit the silk'. The aim was to arrive in one piece back on the airfield.

Immediately the pilot gave the GO signal each trainee pulled his rip cord and the little pilot 'chute' would spring out dragging the main canopy from the pack. It would open with a crack like thunder and wrench the trainee off the wing with a neck-breaking jerk. Pilot Officer Bennett landed off the airfield and had to be retrieved.

By way of a little more exciting entertainment they would partake of squadron gun practice with live ammunition. This was an annual outing and they would all move to Sutton Bridge for the event which had much of the atmosphere of a school sports day. Ground targets were set up on the shores of the Wash.

Siskins had two Vickers guns. These would cease firing at the slightest provocation so the guns were installed with their breech mechanism within easy, spanner-hitting reach of the pilot. They would dive on the targets, wind howling around the open cockpits of the Siskins, bracing wires humming like telephone wires in a gale force wind, guns chattering within a few feet of the pilot's ears. It was all rather more dramatic than effective.

There was an occasion, while flying in a Siskin formation during an exercise south of London when Don Bennett had his only flying accident. Heavy icing conditions were encountered, his airspeed indicator ceased to operate, the turn needle (which was the only gyro instrument fitted in a Siskin) lost its suction because the venturi tube had iced up and then the engine stopped! Carburettor icing or for that matter any form of icing, was little understood at the time. He found a large field but by now the wings had collected a lot of ice, the aircraft sank heavily, broke its undercarriage and went over on to its back. A chastened Don Bennett emerged from the wreckage unhurt.

From his earliest association with flying navigation had fascinated Don Bennett. Many of the techniques in current use had been borrowed from marine practice but new methods, specially adapted for aviation, were being developed all the time. To fly an aircraft and admire the view below may be fun but the aeroplane is a useless toy unless it can be made to arrive at the intended destination. In civil aviation this could be one of the major airports of the world; to the service pilot a typical objective would be to locate a target and destroy it. All this was not lost on the young Pilot Officer Bennett and he moved heaven and earth to get himself onto a navigation course. During the 1930s the only way an RAF pilot could learn about navigation in any depth was to get himself accepted for a flying boat course. This was easier said than done because flying boats, at the time the largest aircraft operated by the Royal Air Force, were virtually a 'closed shop', something of an air force within an air force. Being a determined young man Don Bennett got himself accepted for a flying boat course and a posting to the flying boat station at Calshot soon followed. There were two courses of navigation in progress, the coastal course and the more complex 'long N' course which must have been comprehensive because it took a year to complete. Don Bennett regards Calshot as the turning point in his career.

The seaplane base at Calshot consisted of a few hangars at the end of a spit of land not far from the old castle. The course, which lasted six months, was conducted on Supermarine Southampton flying boats, the early version of which had a wooden hull. Bennett's flying instructor was 'Laddie' Clift, an old sweat of the 'flying boat union', a fraternity that took a pride in their RAF gold wire cap badges, turned green by years of sea spray.

The Southampton was Bennett's first experience of twin-engined aircraft so there was a double transition to face; multi-engine and seaplane handling. The technique of asymmetric flying was barely understood at the time, which is hardly surprising because when an engine failed there was no question of continuing the flight. It was impossible to maintain height on one motor and if one of them failed, a by no means unique event, it was essential to alight on the water without delay. Fortunately the engines were spaced closely together above the hull and within the big, biplane wings. Also there were three large rudders. So there were no minimum control speed problems — it stalled before the pilot ran out of directional control. Don Bennett had a strong affection for marine aircraft. He found them more enjoyable to fly than landplanes.

On the navigation course there was much talk about the new wireless direction finding equipment which was always referred to as "coming soon" whenever it was mentioned during lectures. Dead reckoning and astro navigation were both well taught but this is to be expected; there was a backlog of marine experience to support these branches of navigation. In the event Don Bennett was in his element; he loved flying boats and by now the subject of air navigation was occupying much of his time; to him it was of absorbing interest.

Since he did particularly well at navigation the RAF posted him to 210 Squadron, Pembroke Dock in South West Wales. By now he had a little car and his arrival at the station, with its somewhat grim exterior and in the pouring rain, was at first rather less than encouraging. Once inside the high stone walls surrounding the various buildings a very different picture emerged because Pembroke Dock was a happy station. They flew a later version of the Supermarine Southampton which had a metal hull but later these flying boats were replaced by the somewhat larger Short Singapore. Much of the work at Pembroke Dock entailed night flying and fishery protection duties, something which occupies many of the world's air forces to this day.

It was while he was stationed at Pembroke Dock that the establishment received a new commanding officer, a dynamic and resourceful RAF officer by name of Arthur Harris. Little could Bennett have realised at the time that 'Bert' Harris, as he became known, was to have the most profound influence on his life. Neither could Arthur Harris have foreseen that Bennett, a promising young Australian officer with a thirst for aeronautical knowledge, would many years hence become his indispensable *enfant terrible* at a time when fate had placed him in command of the most powerful bombing force in the history of warfare.

Don Bennett did not stay long at Pembroke Dock; his value had been recognised and very soon the RAF posted him back to Calshot as a flying instructor on the boats he had left. He did not particularly welcome the move but part of the routine entailed flying boat cruises around the British Isles. With him would be two or three student pilots, a wireless operator and one or two maintenance personnel. Reliability being what it was at the time, a load of spares would be carried.

Four or perhaps five flying boats would take part in these training exercises which usually lasted for ten days or so. A typical air cruise would entail stops at Felixstowe, Queensferry (near the Forth Bridge in Scotland), Inverness, Oban, Stranraer, Londonderry (Northern Ireland), Pembroke Dock and Plymouth. Such exercises were conducted by the RAF every three months and at all times of the year. It was the fashion, in aircraft of 1930 vintage, for the pilots to sit in open cockpits and often they would be drenched while on the water.

With engine failures a part of everyday life, and because the Southampton flying boats could not maintain height on one engine, they avoided flying over land whenever possible. On one occasion Don Bennett's flying boat lost power on one engine and they were forced to alight near a destroyer. In the 1930s the Royal

Navy was still fighting a rearguard action directed towards having the RAF dismantled so that they and the Army could share the pieces, consequently it was with some ill-concealed pleasure that a condescending R.N. Commander offered Don Bennett a tow to the nearest harbour. He was not too proud to accept.

A cable fit to tug the QE2 was attached to the little mooring ring in the bow of the Southampton, then the destroyer set off at a sprightly rate of knots. In the stern of the naval ship stood a rating armed with an Aldis lamp. "Can we go any faster?" he signalled. "Tell them certainly not", Bennett ordered his radio operator who promptly started to reply with his signal lamp. Before he could flash the second word the rating disappeared from the stern with 'certainly' written on his message pad and soon the destroyer was steaming hard, bows out of the water, the flying boat on the verge of taking off. These training flights taught Don Bennett a lot about operating marine aircraft under all conditions and within a few years the experience would prove of immense value when the time came for him to seek a new career outside the service. No opportunity to learn something new was ever missed — no lesson, once learned, was ever forgotten.

A combination of talents, the ability to absorb knowledge, his devotion to professionalism and single-mindedness, contributed to the heights he was to attain at a remarkably early age. But fate often played to his advantage. A typical example was his involvement in the McRobertson England to Australia air race of 1934, an event organised to commemorate the centenary of Melbourne. The race was an ambitious affair and it encouraged the de Havilland company to design and build three advanced twin-engined racers, one of which won the event. For its time the Comet was very advanced, it had such features as a retractable undercarriage and variable pitch propellers of a simple kind.

Like many other pilots Don Bennett gave thought to the possibility of taking part. One of the main hurdles was to find a suitable aircraft. A friend, Captain Baird of early Schneider Trophy fame, helped him obtain the loan of a Rolls-Royce engine but all attempts at finding a suitable airframe for it came to nought. In the event Don Bennett had to settle for second best. A fellow Australian by name of Jimmy Woods owned a Lockheed Vega, a high-wing monoplane of portly exterior but advanced concept in some respects. Woods, a pilot of limited experience, would do the flying and Don Bennett was to look after navigation. In retrospect it was not a good arrangement. Woods was obviously short of money and there were technical problems with the aircraft which proved difficult to solve. As the starting date drew near it seemed unlikely that the Vega would be ready. These difficulties Jimmy Woods refused to take seriously, in marked contrast to Don Bennett who worried about the various problems. At a time when Woods should have been supervising the various modifications required for the race he was in London socialising. To him it was all a big joke; Bennett regarded the race with his usual professionalism.

With little time in hand they checked in at RAF Mildenhall, starting point for the race, and at 6.39 am on 20 October the Woods-Bennett team took off on the first leg. The Vega carried no radio and much of the route was over cloud with Woods flying in complete trust of Don Bennett's navigation. Three hours and forty-five minutes later the Lockheed Vega arrived at Marseilles. They flew on to Rome and made for Athens in the dark. One of the technical faults that had plagued the Vega was a seized oleo strut which on occasions would refuse to telescope and absorb shock while on the ground. In the hands of a skilful pilot they might have been able to live with the problem but at Aleppo in Syria, Woods made a heavy landing, the undercarriage collapsed and it was the end of the race for the Vega. Woods suffered no more than minor cuts but Don Bennett collected three crushed vertebrae. Nevertheless within two weeks he was back at Calshot flying his beloved Southampton flying boats.

On the face of it the air race enterprise was bound to fail. Woods, the confirmed amateur who refused to take anything seriously, was not the right companion for Bennett, the totally dedicated professional. However, the purpose of telling this story is to illustrate how fate at times treated Don Bennett kindly. With the race in prospect he decided to study hard and attempt the examinations for one of the toughest civil qualifications at that time, the First Class Navigators Licence.

The 1st N, as it was usually known, entailed a lot of study and hard work, even for an RAAF officer like Bennett who was a navigation instructor at Calshot. The examinations were only ten weeks ahead and study progress was not helped when the Station Commander instigated formal dress for dinner during weekdays. Formal dinner in an RAF officers' mess is, to this day, a leisurely affair but Bennett got around the difficulty by doing without his dinner. Instead he would fry sausages for supper on the open coal fire in his room. That way he was able to work solidly from stand-down until 2am in the morning.

When Don Bennett passed the exams at his first attempt he became one of only seven people in the world to hold a First Class Navigators Licence. The liaison with Jimmy Woods may have put him in hospital for a few days, but it also spurred him on to gain a 1st N.

It is typical of Don Bennett that he should go for the hardest to obtain qualification first, but in his remaining time at Calshot the urge to gain more licences never left him. He obtained a 'B' licence (the professional pilots licence that existed until 1947 when it was replaced by three grades of professional licence). Next he gained a civil wireless operators licence, a flying instructors certificate and not content with that, his ground engineers A, C and X licences which allowed him to carry out maintenance work on airframes, engines and aircraft instruments. The motive for gaining this unprecedented list of aeronautical qualifications may not have been entirely clear to Bennett himself at the time but obviously, with his term of service in the RAF coming to a close, he must have had his eye on a future in civil aviation. And he was determined to be the best qualified applicant when time came to look for a job.

Chapter 4
Imperial Airways

Apart from his unsuccessful participation in the England to Australia air race in 1934, Don Bennett's first real involvement with civil aviation came during his last year of service with the Royal Air Force at Calshot. He would spend his weekends flying for Jersey Airways Ltd, a small, independent airline carrying passengers between Heston, Southampton, Portsmouth and Jersey. They had a fleet of de Havilland Dragons, light, twin-engine biplanes carrying 8-10 passengers.

There was no proper airfield on the island of Jersey in those days so they used the beach. Arrivals and departures were timed to avoid the tides and although the sea never claimed an aircraft the company 'office', an antique bus, was finally swept out on the waves.

It was a good arrangement for all concerned. Bennett was gaining experience, the company enjoyed the services of a highly qualified pilot, he was not being paid and those employed by the company were able to have time off thanks to the relief captain from RAF Calshot. All this came to an end when some pompous gentleman with nothing more important on his mind stood up in the House of Commons and asked if it was true that a serving RAF officer was depriving civil pilots of their living.

One of the squadron commanders at Calshot had living with his family an exceptionally pretty Swiss girl with beautiful blonde hair. She was learning to speak English and, notwithstanding his almost obsessional quest for more and still more qualifications, her presence was not lost on Don Bennett. On 11 August, 1935, his term of engagement at an end, he left the RAAF and, as a consequence the Royal Air Force. Ten days later he married the Swiss girl and now he was a 25-year-old pilot with no job in prospect and a wife to support. He had 1350 hours in his log book on twenty-one types of aircraft. And of course he held probably more licences and ratings than any other pilot in the world. The young Mrs Bennett did not like her first name and she had formed the habit of calling herself Ly (pronounced Lee) which is an abbreviation. Before looking for a job Donald visited Ly's family in Switzerland. Then the couple sailed to Australia so that Ly could meet the Bennett family. From Southampton to Brisbane took six weeks on the *S.S. Hobson's Bay* but there was no hurry, for was the journey not part of their honeymoon? So it would have been for most newly married couples but Don Bennett used some of the time to write the first chapter of his book *The Complete Air Navigator*. He would have written far more but for social activities on board the passenger liner.

The Australian press and the aviation industry 'down under' were nonplussed by Don Bennett's string of qualifications, as well they might be for probably nowhere else in the world was there another pilot who could match the boy from Toowoomba's list of licences and ratings. However, ambitions of working in his own country were soon dashed; despite the best endeavours of those who were anxious for him to stay there was little the Australian aviation industry could offer. For example, the managing director of New England Airways needed a navigation superintendent, a job Bennett could have handled in his sleep, but the salary offered was less than half of what he could earn in the UK. Furthermore, prospects were limited so, rather sadly, he took his wife back to England on a cargo ship, completing his book on the way. He would churn out the words while his beautiful young wife typed the manuscript. The book ran to many editions and it became accepted as an authoritative manual of air navigation.

Back in England it was his ex-Commanding Officer, Arthur Harris, who arranged an interview for him with Imperial Airways. A little should be said about this fine, pioneering airline. In the years immediately following the end of the first World War a number of private aircraft firms began carrying passengers. Air Transport and Travel Ltd was flying between London and Paris in 1919, and Handley Page flew this route as well as London — Brussels. Continental-based airlines were enjoying government subsidies, those in the UK were not, so in the face of impossible competition the British firms were forced to cease operations.

By tradition British governments, almost without exception, have a habit of locking the stable after the horse has bolted. Now that there were no British airlines it was decided to offer a subsidy

Air Vice-Marshal Donald Bennett, DSO

Celia Juliana Bennett, mother of the talented Bennett boys.

Clyde Kinsey Bennett, oldest of the brothers.

Aubrey George Bennett, doctor in the family.

Arnold Lucas Bennett, later to become Sir Arnold, QC.

and follow the example of France, Belgium and Italy. A year was to pass before operations re-started and then short term subsidies were granted to Handley Page Air Transport Ltd (London to Paris), Daimler Hire (London — Manchester — Amsterdam), Instone Air Lines (London — Brussels — Cologne) and British Marine Navigation Co. (Southampton — Channel Isles).

After a few years one of those typically British institutions, the Government Committee, was set up and in 1924 the Hamblin Committee submitted its findings on the future of British airlines. As a result, it was decided to merge the four companies and call it Imperial Airways. The actual formation was on 1st April, 1924 and a wag of the day made the comment that the date was "very appropriate since only fools would want to fly".

Imperial Airways got off to a bad start because the pilots found themselves in dispute with the company. The row continued until Major Brackley, DSO, DSC got the two sides around the table. Brackley, a highly regarded figure on the aviation scene, was made Air Superintendent of Imperial Airways for his efforts. The formation of this great airline was fortuitous for the UK aircraft industry because, for the first time in Britain, aircraft were designed specifically for civil airline use. This had a profound effect on what the passenger had to pay and it is interesting to note that in 1920, when the London — Paris route was being flown with converted Handley Page 0/400 bombers, a one-way ticket cost £25 which was a lot of money at the time. By the late 1930s the fare had dropped to only £4.75.

In 1924 pilots were issued with an Imperial Airways *Pilot's Handbook and General Instructions.* Among the gems in this little publication were — "Rule 3. Stunt landings and stunt takings-off are prohibited". A section devoted to "Forced Landing Instructions" listed the relief landing grounds to be used when engine failure or bad weather made it necessary to terminate the flight. Train times from the nearest station were given — they were a brave race, the fare-paying air passengers of 1924. When gold was carried pilots were issued with a gun.

By the time Don Bennett joined Imperial Airways in January 1936 the airline had twelve years of operating experience behind it and the company was poised to take delivery of the newest and most advanced flying boats in the world. He reported to Major Brackley, the Air Superintendent who had opened up the Empire routes, and the great man sent him to Croydon for three weeks training on the DH 86, a larger, four-engine version of the famous de Havilland Rapide. He also flew the Boulton and Paul

Mailplane. They told Bennett to become current on all types operated by the company so he got himself strapped into the Handley Page 42 and the Short Scylla, both of them massive, four-engine biplanes carrying up to 36 passengers. Not much was required of professional pilots during the nineteen thirties which are often referred to as 'the golden age of flying'. Bennett describes the air test for adding a new aircraft type to your licence as "six landings, three of them heavy"!

Don Bennett's first real airline flight was as First Officer of a Handley Page 42 during a night flight from Croydon to Paris. The captain, an old hand by name of Horsey, had a friend among the passengers, so not long after take-off he handed over to Bennett and disappeared towards the 'gin-and-tonic' area, as the passenger cabin was often known. Approaching Paris Le Bourget airport the captain returned to the flight deck and made the landing. It was only while driving into the town after the flight that a shocked Captain Horsey was acquainted with the fact that this was Bennett's first flight in an HP 42. They made Don Bennett a Captain soon after the Paris trip — those were the days!

With so much of his RAF experience devoted to marine aircraft it was not long before Imperial Airways took Don Bennett off landplanes and sent him to Egypt where he was to fly the Alexandria — Brindisi route on Short Kent flying boats. Sometimes the smaller Short Calcutta was used. These aircraft had a limited range and a miserable 75-knot cruising speed which left nothing in hand when strong headwinds were encountered. Often it was necessary to abandon a flight before the point of no return was reached. This was the period when Italy was at war with defenceless Abyssinia and a toothless League of Nations was imposing meaningless sanctions. The Italians responded by being tiresome to British passengers on overnight stay in Brindisi. Fascist flags were everywhere, larger-than-life characters would whip up 'popular' demonstrations at the slightest provocation and crowds would demonstrate by marching up and down the street outside the hotel used by Imperial Airways for its passengers. Threats made to British passengers were more theatrical than real but there was an occasion when the situation became ugly. An Imperial Airways clerk, tired of the comic opera being enacted outside his room in the street below, registered his lack of appreciation by emptying a jug of water on the crowd from his bedroom window. They put him in gaol. Although it was never proved the loss of Kent flying boat *Sylvanus,* burned out at its moorings, in Brindisi, is believed by many to have been an act of sabotage carried out by Italian Fascists. As a result it was necessary to continue the service with Calcutta flying boats which had been withdrawn from service.

Because a headwind could so profoundly reduce the range of these old boats the service could be delayed for days. There was the particularly bad occasion when weather conditions caused an enforced stay of five days in Brindisi but Don Bennett put the time to good use. He wrote a flying boat handling manual entitled *The Air Mariner.*

It was during Don Bennett's flying boat days with Imperial Airways that world aviation experienced one of those giant leaps forward on the road to progress. British aviation, by tradition a victim of governments without real understanding of the industry and its potential for the good of the nation, had in 1932 suffered a particularly depressing period following the so-called 'Geddes Axe'. This act of political slaughter placed Britain many years behind other countries in terms of civil aviation progress. That was in 1922. Now, ten years later, the first thaw in a bleak winter, partly encouraged by new competition along the air routes from other states, at last urged the British Parliament to safeguard the future of Empire air transport. Sir Alan Cobham had already demonstrated the feasibility of extending the range of aircraft by in-flight refuelling (transferring fuel from a tanker aircraft through a long hose to, for example, a passenger airliner or a freighter). Even earlier, in fact during 1925, he had proved that it was possible to operate flying boats down the Nile, along the continent of Africa to Durban and beyond. Imperial Airways, with Government encouragement, decided to replace its old biplane flying boats with larger, more modern equipment, something that would rival the very successful Sikorski flying boats operated by Pan American Airlines.

Apparently, Arthur Gouge, chief designer at Shorts, was thinking in terms of a new, large biplane but along with some of his directors he witnessed the start of the MacRobertson England to Australia air race. At Mildenhall they saw at close quarters the sleek Douglas DC2 monoplane (forerunner of the legendary DC3, later known as the Dakota). The aircraft was of advanced concept for its time. First it was a monoplane and completely free of bracing wires or struts. It also had retracting main wheels and variable pitch propellers. Furthermore almost the entire airframe was of metal stressed skin construction, fabric covering being confined to the control surfaces.

The DC2 had a profound influence on Shorts. It persuaded the company to say farewell to big biplanes. When it appeared, Arthur Gouge's masterpiece, the S23, was very much in advance of any other flying boat. Even by present day standards it was a large aircraft spanning 114 feet and by the time it entered service with Imperial Airways its maximum take-off weight was 52,500 lbs, twice that of a DC3. From the bows the main deck extended backwards for about 55 feet. Behind the main entrance door the undersurface of the hull had a step so the floor level of the rear cabin was slightly higher than that of the 'promenade cabin'. There was also a smoking cabin/dining room. Early examples carried only 17 passengers in addition to a lot of mail so, in marked contrast to present day travel, each person had a lot of room.

On an upper deck was the radio officer's station, a mail compartment, a fully equipped kitchen and a separate office for the flight clerk. Up front was the spacious flight deck. It was powered by four Bristol Pegasus engines, each of 740 hp but later aircraft had more powerful motors and accommodation for 29 passengers.

Imperial Airways ordered 29 of these magnificent passenger aircraft straight off the drawing board. In the 1930s it was unprecedented for an airline to buy new aircraft before the prototype had flown but faith in the S23 was fully justified when they entered service. At first they were known as 'C' class flying boats but they were quickly introduced on all Empire routes, consequently they were usually referred to as Empire Boats. By the time all long distance routes covered by Imperial Airways were being flown with Empire flying boats, Croydon was confined to European traffic.

The first of the Short Empire Boats was delivered to Imperial Airways on 20 October 1936. It was the policy in those days to assign a flying boat to a particular captain for in many respects the Short S23 was a flying ship. However as traffic increased it rapidly became clear that aircraft were capable of flying more hours per year than their human crews. In air transport the name of the game is 'utilisation', consequently it is not uncommon for modern jet aircraft to fly 3500 hours *per annum*. To keep them in the air six crews per aircraft are needed. To a lesser extent so it was in 1936 and Imperial Airways was soon forced to abandon the attractive idea of one captain to one flying boat.

Naturally there was much jockeying for position among Imperial Airways crews anxious to fly the new Empire Boats. To some extent commands were given on a seniority basis and the first one delivered, named *Canopus*, went to Captain Frank "Bill" Bailey. Somehow or other young Donald Bennett managed to gain command of the fourth S23 delivered, G-ADUX, carrying the name *Cassiopeia*. So at the age of only 26 the youngest of the Bennett family was captain of the 1936 equivalent of a modern Jumbo Jet. It was one of the largest commercial passenger aircraft flying and it offered standards of space and gracious living that, to this day, are talked of with reverence by those fortunate enough to have flown down the Nile in one, or perhaps to the Far East.

First route flown by Imperial Airways new flying boats was from Southampton to Alexandria but it was not long before they were flying in stages to Durban, South Africa and Australia via Singapore. Conditions varied down the Empire routes and at Wadi Halfa mooring could be tricky in the face of strong currents allied to high winds. Bennett witnessed a dreadful incident when a native boy fell off a refuelling barge and was devoured by a crocodile before anything could be done.

It was while the Bennetts were based in Egypt that their daughter Noreen Daphne was born. These were heady days for the young couple. Donald had reached the height of his profession, captain of the finest commercial aircraft flying anywhere in the world. And he was still in his mid-twenties.

The Empire Boats gave great confidence to their passengers. There was nothing of the stick-and-wire about them and as the motor launch drew alongside with a load of long distance travellers they would look up at a towering, riveted hull which seemed more like an ocean-going liner than the fabric covered, wire braced biplanes still being used on some of the overland routes. In the main flying the Empire Boats offered new standards of safety and reliability to passengers and crews alike. But there were 'those moments'. Like the time Don Bennett was taking-off from the Hooghly River, Calcutta. It was a hot, windless day and the water was like glass, clinging to the hull of the flying boat and refusing to yield the great aluminium bird to the sky. After a long, protracted run across the water they finally unstuck to be confronted by the Willingdon Bridge, a large and remarkably solid looking edifice. There was not enough room to climb over it — so Bennett flew underneath.

On another occasion of a different kind Don Bennett experienced particularly strong tailwinds while flying from Egypt to England. Alexandria to Southampton had never previously been flown non-stop but conditions were favourable and as they crossed over France the excited passengers were at frequent intervals given up-to-the-minute ground speeds. They landed at Southampton with twenty minutes of daylight in hand.

Naturally, other airlines were anxious to buy the Short S23 and while Don Bennett was converting Imperial Airways pilots on to the big boats his schoolboy hero, Lester Brain, by now with Qantas the Australian airline, flew with him down the African route to Durban. The great man was soon to fly Empire Boats for Qantas and the airline had sent him to Imperial Airways for some first-hand experience.

Although the Empire Boats were well in advance of anything flying at the time there were accidents on the routes although these were usually caused through lack of operational experience rather than mechanical malfunction. However one problem remained — lack of range. This was not peculiar to the Short flying boats; it was a limiting factor with all aircraft of the period. The problem was simply that engines in the 1930s were not powerful enough to fly a commercial load with sufficient fuel for, to quote an example, an Atlantic crossing. The early Empire Boats were unable to make the trip even when no passengers or freight were carried. Yet there was a pressing need for long distance mail flights and an Atlantic passenger service, one of mankind's ambitions since the first days of flight, was in the 1930s a task almost equivalent to putting a man on the moon. Various ideas were being tried. Sir Alan Cobham's flight refuelling was used for a short while although it has since found its main application with military aircraft. Lufthansa, the German airline, experimented with large refuelling barges anchored at suitable places in the Atlantic. Their flying boats would land, refuel and then be catapulted off the barge in an overloaded condition. Hardly surprisingly the exercise was disliked by the German pilots who were subjected to an acceleration of more than 4g. In any case the Lufthansa method could only be used for mail or freight. Fare-paying passengers would be unlikely to try the experience twice.

General Manager (Technical) at Imperial Airways during the period was Major Robert Mayo, at one time a professional test pilot. He proposed lifting an overloaded mailplane into the air on the back of a powerful but lightly loaded carrier aircraft. At cruising altitude the two aircraft would separate, the carrier returning to base while the mailplane, carrying more fuel than it could lift off the water under its own power, would speed non-stop to its destination. The idea was not entirely new. A similar experiment had taken place in 1916 when a small flying boat named the *Porte Baby* successfully lifted a Bristol Scout fighter, the two aircraft separating at a safe height.

In 1935 the entire project was estimated to cost only £60,000 — less than the price of a modern light twin-engined aircraft. An order was placed with Shorts who used a modified Empire Boat for the carrier 'plane and a four-engine floatplane of new design called *Mercury* acted as mailplane. The carrier was named *Maia* and the project created worldwide excitement in aviation circles as well as in the lay Press.

By the time the Mayo composite aircraft project had been translated into hardware an improved, more powerful version of the Empire Boats, called the S30, was under development for the Atlantic run using flight refuelling to obtain the necessary range but much development work was needed to ensure rendezvous of the two aircraft with total certainty. Don Bennett was quick to appreciate the possibilities of the Mayo project and, true to form, he immediately asked if he could join the development team which had been set up at Imperial Airways.

Major Mayo was a tall, rather shy man of considerable ability. He readily agreed to Don Bennett joining his exclusive, high-powered department. Once again he had positioned himself at the forefront of aviation technology. There was a lot more to the Mayo concept than a big aircraft helping a small, over-loaded one off the water. At low speeds most of the weight was carried by the large carrier 'plane but as speed increased *Mercury* took over more and more of the total weight until it partly supported *Maia*. *Mercury* rested on *Maia*, being located on six spherical knobs which registered in suitable cups built into the structure. A single hook, made up of three elements, held the two aircraft together. So long as the two aircraft were locked together the pilot of *Mercury* was unable to move his flying controls. There was a barometric safety device which prevented inadvertent separation of the aircraft at too low an altitude. Both pilots were provided with instruments reading the pulling force between aircraft and a system of lights warned the pilots when this was insufficient to ensure positive separation. A telephone link between pilots safeguarded the operation against misunderstanding through lack of communication and when the instruments read 'all systems go' the lower pilot pulled his release lever. This removed one element of the attachment hook. Next the pilot of *Mercury* pulled his release and that left the third hook element, a spring loaded device which parted when a pull of 5000 lbs or more existed between aircraft. At that point the aircraft separated, *Maia* entering a gentle descent while an overloaded *Mercury* staggered into the climb.

Mercury was a floatplane, 73 feet in span. Empty it weighed 10,000 lbs but when fully loaded with mail and fuel it turned the scales at 20,800 lbs. At that weight it was incapable of taking-off under its own power (four Napier-Halford engines). However, with the aid of *Maia* it could fly with 1200 Imperial gallons of fuel and carry a ton of payload over an unprecedented non-stop 3800 statute miles. After the two aircraft had been individually tested the first coupled flight occurred on 20 January 1938. On 6 February the first separation was made with complete success. Many years later, when the Americans were conducting experiments with their Apollo space shuttle, which is carried aloft on the back of a large rocket and ferried on top of a Jumbo Jet, they were gracious enough to put up notices in the factory which said "Remember, the Brits did it first."

Following certification the Mayo composite aircraft was handed over to Imperial Airways. Fuel consumption trials took up much time with Don Bennett at the controls of *Mercury* and Captain Wilcockson in the carrier aircraft. The spring of 1938 was an eventful time for Bennett. On 28 May his son, Torix Peter was born. Then he became involved in preparations for some remarkable record breaking flights in *Mercury*. It was during these proving flights that he almost lost his life in a silly accident. At 5 am one morning Bennett had climbed on top of *Maia* in preparation for entering *Mercury*. In his hand were a sextant and some charts. There was a patch of oil on the wing, he slipped and fell more than twenty feet into the water. Fortunately the motor launch which had just brought him out was no longer there, otherwise he might have broken his back. They fished him out of the water, still clutching his precious sextant which had been specially made to his design by Kelvin Hughes, the famous instrument manufacturers.

There had been some pessimistic fuel consumption figures quoted by one or two of the pilots engaged in the *Mercury* project. Bennett was of the opinion that they were not using the mixture controls correctly and, to the surprise of some and annoyance of others, he proved his point on a long distance flight over the ocean. Because of this he was entrusted with the first commercial flight across the Atlantic. On 20 July, 1938 the *Mercury/Maia* composite took off and separated over Foynes, the seaplane base near Limerick, Southern Ireland. *Mercury* was carrying 600 lbs of newspapers and newsreels and it flew non-stop to Montreal, a distance of 2930 miles covered in 20 hours 20 minutes, then down to New York. The American press went wild, banner headlines swamped the newspapers and Don Bennett was photographed with the Rockettes, the famous dancing girls who performed at Radio City.

Manager of Imperial Airways New York office from 1929 until his retirement in 1963 was Paul Bewshea and he remembers meeting Don Bennett after his arrival.

"He was as fresh as paint after the long flight but Coster [the radio operator accompanying Bennett] went flat out on his bed in the suite I had got in the Hotel Shelton. Don sat with me and planned his return flight, telling me the exact route (Botwood Newfoundland, Azores to Southampton) and said he would arrive on the exact date on which he did. He then went to bed."

Such was the impact of Bennett's flight across the Atlantic with a commercial load that he now had the ear of people in high places. Others had broken records but some of them had a drink problem or were difficult and unreliable to deal with. Here was a young man, only twenty-eight-years old, who was a professional to his finger tips — and he did not drink or smoke! So when Don Bennett suggested to the Air Minister (at the time Sir Kingsley Wood) that he should be allowed to make an attempt on the world long distance seaplane record the idea was readily accepted.

Shorts modified the floats to carry additional fuel and it was then decided to go for the world's absolute long distance record. The composite was moved to Dundee in Scotland on 21 September and they aimed at flying to Cape Town, non-stop. First officer/radio operator accompanying Don Bennett was Ian Harvey. This was the time of the Munich crisis and at one stage, with the possibility of war on everyone's mind, it seemed likely the project would be cancelled. However on 6 October 1938 *Mercury* took on board another 2000 gallons of fuel to fill the tanks weight was then 27,500 lbs. The composite took off, all eight engines at maximum power. Separation occurred at 4700 feet and Bennett set course for Capt Town. At their very high weight, 7000 lbs heavier than during the Atlantic crossing, more power was needed for the cruise than had been anticipated. In fact, for the first twelve hours the engines were at full throttle.

For best economy they had planned a 10,000-foot cruise but icing conditions over southern England forced them to descend and continue the flight at 3000 feet where fuel consumption was high. Then soon afterwards an engine cowling shed one panel, increasing drag in the process.

Ten hours after take-off *Mercury* crossed the Algerian coast. Then came the formidable Atlas mountains, strong headwinds and tropical thunderstorms as they flew on towards the Equator. Matters were not exactly going according to plan for Captain Bennett and First Officer Harvey. The situation was made even worse when the electric pump system refused to transfer fuel from the floats to the main tanks. An emergency hand pump had been provided but at 12,000 feet without oxygen the task of moving 1400 gallons of fuel demands a lot of energy. Bennett and Harvey took it in turns to man the pump but at one time it looked as though it would be impossible to transfer enough fuel to allow a second night in the air. Naturally as petrol was used and the aircraft became lighter so engine power could be reduced and the fuel flow diminished accordingly. It was rather like the old joke about the village garage proprietor who was trying to fill a large Rolls-Royce which was quietly ticking over as he worked the pump. "Would you mind switching off so that I can catch up" he asked the car owner. So it was in *Mercury*. At one time Don Bennett left Harvey at the controls to monitor the instruments and keep an eye on the autopilot. He returned to find an empty flight deck. Harvey was on his seat at the radio installation and suffering from hallucinations. "Where is the other chap?" he demanded of Bennett, "He has gone — I know he has gone." After the flight he remembered imagining a third, non-existent crew member.

A combination of headwinds and excess drag from the damaged engine cowling put Cape Town out of reach but down below was the Orange River and they alighted near the Alexander Bay Diamond mines having broken the long distance record for seaplanes. Actual distance flown was 6045 miles but records of this kind are assessed in a straight line so the FAI recorded it as 5997.5 miles flown non-stop in 42.5 hours.

By any standards it had been an astonished flight yet although it represented an important milestone in world aviation Bennett and his co-pilot were not given so much as a works luncheon party by Shorts or even a cocktail party by Imperial Airways. Bennett made a number of revenue flights in *Mercury*. One entailed flying a ton of Christmas mail from Southampton to Alexandria. When war broke out in September the following year *Mercury* was handed over to No. 320 Netherlands Squadron where it was flown by Dutch pilots who had managed to get out to Holland when the Germans invaded the Low Countries. It is sad to record that in 1941 this remarkable and historic aircraft was flown back to Shorts at Rochester where it was broken up.

In June 1939 Parliament introduced a Bill aimed at forming British Overseas Airways by amalgamating Imperial Airways with British Airways. It passed its second reading in the House of Commons with a majority of 79. On 4 August Royal Assent was given to the Bill and the merger took place on 1 April 1940, seven months after the start of World War II. Imperial Airways always supported the British aircraft industry. That would end under the new regime.

It is worth recording that when British Airways (which had never made any money) merged with Imperial Airways (which had consistently shown modest profits) an ungrateful Conservative government refused to recommend any honours for the pioneers who had done so much for British and world aviation. And these same politicians, who had watched with unseeing eyes events in a Germany gone mad, were finally driven to honour their undertaking and declare war on Hitler when he invaded Poland. The boy from Toowoomba was still only 29 when hostilities began. He had every civil aviation qualification in the book, he had flown the biggest, best and most advanced aircraft as a professional pilot and he held several world records. In September 1939 who could have realised that his remarkable career was only just about to enter its most important phase.

Chapter 5
The Atlantic Ferry

By the time the true nature of Hitler's Germany had percolated through the dusty corridors of Whitehall, and a timid British government had awoken to the facts of the situation, it rapidly became clear that the ancient biplanes of the RAF would be no match for the fast and efficient monoplane fighters of the Luftwaffe. The British are not, by nature, a warlike nation. It takes a lot to provoke them. And its politicians sometimes misjudge a situation because of another national problem — a tendency to imagine that other populations, French, Spanish, Russians or Argentinians, think like Englishmen. They do not. Furthermore different nations are impressed by totally different things.

The damage to Britain's security through not taking a firm stand against Hitler at a time when his ambitions could have been checked and even stopped was twofold. First the world regarded Britain and its Commonwealth as a spent force, ripe for the picking. And secondly the Army, Air Force and to a much lesser extent the Navy, were not in a fit state to defend Britain and its then very considerable Empire.

In so far as the Royal Air Force is concerned expansion did not really get under way until 1935 and then it was largely a matter of increasing the number of trained personnel. True the Hurricane and the Spitfire were in being but these were purely defensive. As an offensive force the RAF was blighted with such aircraft as the Fairey Battle (an underpowered light bomber which was to be shot out of the sky when the fighting started), the Bristol Blenheim (good in its day but obsolete when the war began), the Handley Page Hampden (of limited bomb load with not much performance) and the Armstrong Whitworth Whitley. This was a slow but reliable twin-engined bomber which, until the Vickers Wellington arrived, represented the heaviest punch the RAF could deliver.

What politicians seem unable to comprehend is that if you neglect a country's defences to the point where a potential enemy has the capability of walking in and taking over, snapping fingers and issuing instructions to re-arm with all speed will provide no quick remedy. Factories have to be built, staff must be trained, new tanks, guns, aircraft and ships must be designed, prototypes hand-made, tested and approved before production can start. All this may take four years or more before the weapons start rolling off the lines in meaningful numbers.

When war with Germany seemed unavoidable and the full realisation of Britain's defencelessness hit its sadder but wiser Parliament, desperate steps were taken to purchase aircraft from the USA. There was an urgent need for coastal defence aircraft to replace the ageing Avro Anson with its mechanically-operated, wind-up undercarriage and general lack of capabilities. The RAF purchasing commission did a tour of the American aircraft industry and, among other equipment, ordered the four-engined B24 Liberator bomber, the somewhat older Boeing B17 Flying Fortress and a military version of the Lockheed 14 light airliner. As a civil aircraft it was being used by such airlines as British Airways and KLM, the Dutch company. Fitted with a gun turret and other weapons it became the Hudson. In peacetime it was a relatively straightforward task to ship the wings, fuselages, engines etc. in crates and have them assembled at Speke Airport, Liverpool. But when the shooting started and the U-boats began their plunder of the seas an unacceptably high proportion of these valuable aircraft found their way to the bed of the Atlantic instead of the squadrons of the RAF.

Meanwhile, what of Don Bennett? A month before the war started he was employed on the Atlantic service being flown by the newly formed BOAC. By then the higher powered S30 had replaced the earlier Empire boats and, to ensure adequate range for an Atlantic crossing while carrying a commercial load, in-flight refuelling was being used.

On 3 September 1939 Don Bennett was driving to the flying boat base at Southampton when Prime Minister Neville Chamberlain made his uninspiring declaration to the nation — Britain was at war with Nazi Germany. It was a pitiful admission of failure following his many years of appeasement. This historic broadcast to the British people has been described by many writers in different ways but perhaps the most accurate is in Marshal of the Royal Air Force, Sir Arthur Harris's book *Bomber Offensive.* In it his says Chamberlain "was about as stirring as a schoolmaster confirming that mumps had broken out in a prep school."

On his way across the Atlantic Bennett's radio officer passed him a message he had just received — the *Athenia*, a ship full of women and children on their way to the USA, had just been sunk by a U-boat. The Germans had revealed the way they intended to fight the war. Soon afterwards Bennett was sent to pick up BOAC staff stationed in Italy and after the fall of France he was ordered to take General Sikorski and alight on the water at Biscarosse, near Bordeaux. Remnants of the Polish army were isolated in that part of France; Sikorski aimed at collecting the Polish general staff and bringing it back to Britain.

Don Bennett managed to get the big S30 onto a part of the beach where it was hidden by trees and unlikely to be seen by the Germans who were rounding up units of the French Army. At dawn the next morning four overloaded cars arrived with the Poles, they got on board the BOAC flying boat and soon after take-off a British cruiser shot at them, fortunately without effect. The Royal Navy was not very good at aircraft recognition in those days, or, for that matter, at any time during the war. Their policy seems to have been 'if it's got wings — shoot'.

A week later Don Bennett flew H.R.H. The Duke of Kent to an international trade fair at Lisbon. This was a PR excercise intended to demonstrate that Britain would go about its business, war or no war. At the time, Lisbon was a happy hunting ground for the spies of all nations so, to spread a little confusion and confound the Luftwaffe, Captain Bennett, BOAC, filed a flight plan to West Africa, took off in the dark, flew south west and then turned towards England when out of sight. They landed at Poole, near Bournemouth on 2 July 1940. It was to be Bennett's last flight with the airline.

By this time the U-boat packs were seriously threatening Britain's lifeline with the USA. The Atlantic air service was in its infancy, aircraft were incapable of making the journey with heavy loads and ships were vital if vulnerable. The supply of warplanes to an ill-equipped Royal Air Force was also threatened but there was another way of delivering these to Britain. Lord Beaverbrook, dynamic owner of the *Daily Express,* had been made Minister of Aircraft Production and he pressed for the obvious — fly the American aircraft to Britain under their own power and on their own wings. The experts were consulted, civil and military, among them Air Chief Marshal 'Ginger' Bowhill, C-in-C of Coastal Command. All were of the same opinion —

you cannot deliver aircraft across the Atlantic during the months of winter.

Someone must have mentioned Captain Don Bennett to Beaverbrook because one day the lad from Toowoomba was sent for and ordered to present himself at the Millbank office where the daily firework display was enacted.

"Can you deliver aircraft across the Atlantic"? snarled the great man.

"Suitable ones, yes" replied Bennett.

"But they say you will ice up" countered the Minister of Aircraft Production, eyeing Bennett with suspicion.

"No we won't", insisted Bennett, "We've got Killfrost, [a paste smeared on the flying surfaces which prevents serious formation of ice] and we know one or two things".

All this seemed to impress Beaverbrook because he barked "Well, get out there and start it" to which Bennett replied, "I'll get ready immediately".

"No you won't" retorted Beaverbrook, "You will go now!"

Don Bennett regarded the bullying as all part of an act and he got to like Beaverbrook very much although many of the senior RAF officers were not so enthusiastic about his somewhat unique methods.

Over in Canada the pieces of Beaverbrook's jigsaw puzzle were gradually falling into place. Being an important Canadian he naturally had friends in high places and one of these, in fact the President of the Royal Bank of Canada, put Bennett and his colleagues in touch with the Chairman of Canadian Pacific Railways who had already undertaken to provide administrative back-up for the new enterprise which soon became known as Atlantic Ferry. Operational base was at St. Hubert, later Dorval Airport. Woods Humphreys, ex-managing director of Imperial Airways was placed in charge of the operation, Colonel Burchell, another Imperial Airways man, was appointed general manager and Don Bennett, as yet only 29 years old, was to be Flying Superintendent. The Americans were not yet in the war, consequently Atlantic Ferry had a vital role to perform in seeing that the RAF got its American aircraft.

Bennett lost no time in visiting the Lockheed factory in California and there he went over the Hudson, rivet by rivet, in a way that astonished the Americans. 200 had been ordered by the RAF, initially as navigation trainers but later they performed anti-submarine duties, a job for which they were well suited. Before these light airliners could be used by the RAF a transparent nose had to be fitted with two forward-firing guns along with a bomb bay capable of carrying 750 lbs of stores (bombs, depth charges etc.). Later this was increased to 1000 lbs. When the aircraft arrived at Speke a power-operated gun turret was added. A Hudson of 224 squadron made history by becoming the first RAF aircraft to shoot down a German 'plane during World War II (a Dornier Do18 flying boat which it encountered over Jutland).

The American's first intimation that in Bennett they were dealing with no amateur came when Don refused to accept the manufacturers performance figures. He insisted on starting at dawn, flying a long range fuel consumption test and logging every reading with his usual persistence. The Hudson was pleasant enough to fly but he found that it was about 8 percent down on performance. In consequence, extra fuel would be needed if these aircraft were to be flown across the Atlantic. To the credit of Lockheed the management not only had the grace to accept his findings; they also valued his opinions on the possible reasons for this shortfall in performance. These eminated from a number of sources — some airframe, others engine/propeller. With typical Yankee 'get-up-and-go' they had installed an extra, custom-made fuel tank by the following morning! Had anyone other than Bennett made that factory visit it is interesting to speculate how many Hudsons might have run out of fuel and ditched in the Atlantic before reaching England.

In the main the Hudsons did a good job of work with the RAF. On one occasion three Hudsons attacked no fewer than 40 Junkers Ju87 dive bombers, shooting down five of them and damaging others. They harassed German troops on the ground during the Dunkirk evacuations and some years later Hudsons flew from RAF Tempsford, ferrying agents into and out of France at night with no more than a few dim lights to act as a flarepath. One belonging to 269 Squadron forced U-boat U570 to surrender following an attack. In May 1943 another Hudson sank a U-boat with rocket fire. While these incidents may not be entirely relevant in a biography of Donald Bennett they nevertheless illustrate the importance and value of his work in planning and operating the Atlantic Ferry.

The provision of suitably qualified pilots was bound to present difficulties. It should be remembered that in 1940 the most competent pilots were testing aircraft at the factories, maintaining essential air routes and leading the flights, squadrons, wings and groups of the RAF. Few people had

Captain Don Bennett (left) and crew with Imperial Airways Empire flying boat 'Cabot' on the second trans-Atlantic mail run which was flown on 12 August, 1938. Included in the cargo were 9 brace of grouse for President Roosevelt.

Atlantic Ferry Pilot Memorial erected at Gander, Newfoundland and opened by Don Bennett on 25 October, 1967. The aircraft built into the stone base is a real Lockheed Hudson, the first type to be ferried to England during World War 2.

The Handley Page Hampden, obsolete at the start of the war, nevertheless made its contribution to the early bombing raids.

Strong, dependable but slow. The Armstrong Whitworth Whitley was being flown by No. 77 Squadron when Don Bennett took over as Commanding Officer on re-joining the RAF.

actually flown the Atlantic, certainly not in the winter, and the task of employing, then training pilots, many of them throw-outs from the airlines or the US aircraft industry, placed a heavy burden on the young shoulders of Don Bennett. Some of the 'talent' at his disposal had lost their jobs through persistent drunkenness but, at Beaverbrook's insistence, very high rates of pay were offered to the Americans and this naturally caused friction when first class BOAC captains, responsible people with a lot of flying experience, found themselves doing the same job as the throw-outs but at a fraction of the salary. This was to prove a growing source of discontent. Bennett resented it because better pilots could have been obtained without resorting to bribery of this kind.

Civil pilots were required to have at least 750 hours flying experience, a professional pilots licence and an instrument rating. Training for the Atlantic crossing started immediately after the first two Hudsons were delivered by Lockheed to Atlantic Ferry. Although in many respects it was an excellent aircraft the Hudson was no respecter of fools. Another American aircraft in the pipeline for delivery by the Atlantic Ferry team was the B24 Liberator, a four-engined bomber built by the Consolidated Aircraft Corporation. The B24 had a very long range for the period although its bomb load was poor compared with the British heavy bombers. From the same manufacturer came the Catalina, a twin-engined amphibian which had a then phenomenal range of 4000 miles.

After a period of three months the odd assortment of pilots, some in the smart attire of the airlines, others in anything from flashy shirts to cowboy hats and high-heeled boots, had finished an intensive course in navigation. Even so Bennett thought it prudent to appoint a senior pilot as leader, the others following in loose formation. To keep a delivery together bright station-keeping lights were fitted to the Hudsons. The first delivery of seven Hudsons assembled at Gander, Newfoundland and made ready for the crossing. During the night the aircraft became covered in ice and heavy snow, consequently valuable time was lost in clearing the flying surfaces.

On 10 November 1940 the delivery took off for England with Bennett in the lead aircraft, the other six Hudsons clustered around him at a discreet distance. The Atlantic had never before been crossed so late in the year by a single aircraft, let alone a formation of seven and early in the trip Don Bennett decided to let his Texan co-pilot fly so that he could concentrate on navigating his valuable formation. About three-quarters of the way over they ran into thick cloud. To avoid risk of collision the formation separated and reverted to a flight plan, which Bennett had issued beforehand, as they droned on into the dark, Atlantic night. In the hours that followed Bennett was kept busy checking the progress of his Hudson but in the few moments of relaxation he had much to ponder. How many of his flock had any idea of their position? Were any of them hopelessly lost? Did all the pilots know how to cope with severe ice should it be encountered? Had there been any engine failures? These were anxious questions for a young man to ask himself. For the responsibility was his, and his alone. He, it was, who assured Lord Beaverbrook that the Atlantic Ferry was possible. And he, it was, who gave this advice in the knowledge that he was contradicting most of the others consulted by the Minister of Aircraft Production.

Off the coast of Ireland dawn came to reveal broken cloud below as Bennett descended into clear weather. They joined the circuit at Aldergrove airfield (Belfast) to find another Hudson ahead of them. Well at least two aircraft had made the journey! Soon after landing another three could be seen on the horizon. Then followed an agonizing delay and it seemed as though only five of the original seven had made the crossing. As a message came through telling Bennett that one of his Hudsons had landed at another airfield the last one arrived at Aldergrove. The first Atlantic Ferry, flown late in the year without experienced aircrews, had been a complete success.

Bennett was nevertheless unhappy with the existing arrangements. Formation flying over the Atlantic under winter conditions, with only one specialist navigator in the leading aircraft was too risky. The fact that a second formation led by Humphrey Page and a third commanded by Gordon Store, both of them BOAC captains, had been equally successful could not disguise the situation and its potential dangers. However, Beaverbrook was the kind of man who recognised only two things, success or failure, and he was not prepared to concern himself with the details. Bennett had dug a hole for himself and he was standing on the edge at risk of falling in.

To some extent his position was strengthened by the temporary loan of some first class BOAC captains, many of them ex-Imperial Airways staff, such as 'Taffy' Powell and Gordon Store, both holders of 1st Class Navigator's licences. Then there was A. L. Messenger, Moll (the famous KLM captain who flew the DC2 airliner into second place on the England-Australia air race) and the legendary Captain O. P. Jones, he of the trim beard and white silk gloves who is generally regarded as having done so much for the status of airline pilots. Gordon Store, a South African, had been involved in the early flight refuelling development trials. He was an experienced Imperial Airways, and later, BOAC pilot. During the fighting that followed the German invasion of Norway he was sent to Bodo (south of Narvik) in command of a Short S30 boat filled with experts who were to try and establish a fighter airstrip and radar sites. His, and an accompanying flying boat were both sunk, Gordon Store was shot in the foot and he was lucky to get home.

While convalescing Store asked to be given a Hudson ferry assignment. He was flown across to Canada with Kelly Rogers (the famous Irish airline captain). In the aircraft was Billy Bishop VC, the well known World War I fighter pilot.

Store had known Don Bennett from his airline days and while they were very different in character, each was a professional in his own way. Store often disagreed with the young Australian's methods although he admired his courage and genius. He remembers well those days with the Atlantic Ferry Organisation. The pilots on his delivery were living in a train waiting for the Hudsons to be dug out of the snow. He was to lead the third formation but it very nearly turned into a non-event because the night before take-off the pilots got drunk and there was a fight. During the flight oxygen was fed to the crews through a tube in the mouth — there were no masks or regulators to respond according to the pilot's breathing.

At 15,000 feet they flew on above cloud until an occluded front blocked the way and forced the Hudsons up to 21,000 feet, collecting ice on the way. Store took an astro shot on Polaris and was dismayed to find that the loose gaggle of aircraft was many miles too far north; a forty-five degree heading alteration was needed! The Atlantic wind pattern was little understood in the early days of the war and drift corrections could be enormous. Nevertheless all except one of Store's Hudsons landed at Aldergrove and the other one arrived safely at Prestwick. At that stage Gordon Store transferred to the Royal Air Force but recognising his value as an Atlantic ferry pilot it was not long before the authorities were shipping him back to Canada with instructions to ferry B17 and B24 bombers. He was met in Montreal by Don Bennett who told him "You've had it mate — you are out of the Air Force — I want you as a base commander". This was in fact the second time he had joined and left the RAF in a matter of only three or four months. He was beginning to wonder whether he was a civil pilot or an RAF officer.

Atlantic Ferry continued to operate with civil and RAF crews who made the one-way trip to Britain and were then flown back to Canada by BOAC. By this time the vast Empire Air Training Scheme was well established and many young aircrew were at the various flying schools in Canada. Some of the newly trained navigators found themselves posted to the Atlantic Ferry Organisation where they were placed in the care of Don Bennett. Pilot Officer G. M. Dickson (later Squadron Leader) and his friend P/O Peter Roberts were among the young navigators to meet up with the Master Navigator in person. They hung around Montreal, spending their time on practice plotting across the Atlantic, generally becoming more and more frustrated because they wanted to get into the war. The weeks went by and following a not very friendly meeting with Captain D. C. T. Bennett it was agreed that they should be released and sent home by ship.

They boarded at Halifax. Around them were the other ships which formed the convoy. On deck were some of the Hudsons they had been waiting to navigate across the Atlantic. For some reason there had been a change of plan. On the way over U-boats picked off a number of the freighters which sank taking many of the Hudsons below the waves. It was a convincing demonstration of the need for Atlantic Ferry. About a year later, when Bennett was in the RAF these two by now more experienced navigators found that he was their new squadron commander. "What, not you two" were his opening words when they met in the mess, "I hope you will not want to leave me again this time"!

For the young RAF navigators, fresh out of training school, the Atlantic crossing was a one-way trip. It also made them members of what was then a quite exclusive fraternity; those who had flown the Atlantic. In December 1940 Don Bennett led another formation of aircraft on the delivery run. One departed the runway and was damaged during take-off. Another had to turn back when over the Atlantic because a mechanical problem had developed. By then Bennett's first hand experience of the operation enabled him to speak with authority and he told Beaverbrook that it was the end of the road for 'follow-my-leader' tactics across the ocean. All subsequent Atlantic deliveries were on an individual basis, each aircraft carrying an RAF navigator.

With Liberator, Fortress and Catalina aircraft to deliver as well as the Hudsons, Atlantic Ferry was becoming a very large operation. Jealous eyes cast envious looks at what by any standards had developed into an efficient organisation. There was political intrigue, good people were dismissed and, too often, they were replaced by the incompetent. Bennett, never slow to express his displeasure when unjust and foolish decisions are made, had his moments of friction with those responsible for promoting fools to high places.

How long he would have continued as Superintendent of Flying in an organisation being undermined from within we shall never know. Because on Sunday, 7 December, 1941, at the very time when her diplomats were in discussion with the Americans, Japan launched an unprovoked attack against Pearl Harbour, destroying most of the US Pacific fleet based on the island. America was now at war alongside the British Commonwealth and the various free forces that had managed to fight on after the collapse of their respective countries.

Almost immediately the US Air Force made a bid to control Atlantic Ferry and so did the Canadians. It was agreed that the Americans should assume responsibility for delivering new aircraft from the factories to Montreal. But to stop further attempts at controlling what Britain regarded as a vital service to the war effort Atlantic Ferry ceased to be civil organisation and in July 1941 it was placed under the command of Air Chief Marshal Sir Frederick Bowhill, one of the advisors who had told Beaverbrook that aircraft could not be delivered across the Atlantic in winter. He is even reputed to have described the idea as 'an act of suicide'. Generally, the Air Ministry had been against the setting up of Atlantic Ferry and Beaverbrook, with the support of the Ministry of Aircraft Production, had gone ahead with the project mainly on the advice of Don Bennett. Of the very senior RAF officers who had opposed the Atlantic Ferry in 1940 Bennett will now only comment that 'at the time they knew no better'. It could, of course, be argued that they should have known better or at least have been able to match the knowledge and judgement of a 30-year-old airline captain. But Don Bennett was a professional and the pre-war RAF high command was tainted with more than a trace of in-bred amateurism.

While flying operations at Atlantic Ferry Organisation (known at the time as ATFERO) were under the control of Bennett, hardly any aircraft were lost although there were minor accidents. After he left, in fact during the six weeks following his departure, 3 Liberator bombers, four-engined long range aircraft urgently needed by the RAF, flew into cloud covered mountains killing all on board and six Hudsons disappeared somewhere in the Atlantic. Why the Hudsons were lost will never be known with certainty but the most likely cause was carburettor icing followed by engine failure. Because immediately following his departure from Montreal Bennett's instructions on avoiding carburettor icing were replaced by new ones giving potentialy dangerous advice. One of the prime rules in any successful enterprise is to leave well alone that which is working successfully. The new, high powered management at Montreal obviously thought they knew better than Donald Bennett, first class navigator and master airman. In this they were very much mistaken.

Chapter 6
Back in the Royal Air Force

When Air Chief Marshal Sir Frederick Bowhill took over from the Atlantic Ferry management he told Bennett that, prior to his leaving England, arrangements had been made with the Air Ministry which should secure his re-appointment in the R.A.F. with the rank of Group Captain. Back in England Don Bennett went to see his old chief only to find Beaverbrook packing up his office.

"I'm sacked, so you're sacked" roared the Beaver, "But you've done well and if I am ever again in a position to do so I'll see that you're rewarded". There was to be no recognition for the valuable work Bennett had done in setting up the delivery of aircraft across the Atlantic but it was only the end of a chapter. Another was due to begin.

An appointment had been arranged with Sir Guy Garrod, Air Member for Personnel at the Air Ministry. The gentleman firmly but courteously passed Don Bennett to some relatively junior civil servant who explained that it was quite impossible for the RAF to appoint an ex-airline captain in the rank of Group Captain. Six weeks went by while Bennett tried to re-join the Royal Air Force. First they talked about making him an acting Group Captain, then it was to be acting Wing Commander. When finally he was offered the rank of Squadron Leader (Major, in Army terms) Bennett did some forthright talking and the faceless wonders at the Air Ministry relented to the extent that he was made a Wing Commander and posted to Eastbourne as second-in-command of a new school for navigators capable of training 2000 students at a time. It was a waste of Bennett's unique experience but at least he was back with the old firm.

The navigation school had been set up in Eastbourne College. Initially there was a somewhat cool relationship between Bennett and his commanding officer, an older man who apparently resented the ex-airline captain's lack of medals. The fact that on re-joining the service Bennett had some 8500 hours flying behind him (few RAF pilots had logged more than 2000 hours in those days) was obviously lost on this worthy. Clearly the Eastbourne navigation school was unlikely to provide a suitable outlet for the master pilot's talents so it was not long before Bennett visited Group Captain "Daddy" Dowes, personnel officer at Bomber Command Headquarters. It did not take the old veteran more than a few moments to recognise what the young Wing Commander had to offer and Bennett was immediately appointed Commanding Officer of 77 Squadron of 4 Group which was commanded by an old colleague, Air Vice-Marshal Carr. 'Roddy' Carr had been Air Officer Commanding Northern Ireland while Bennett was running the flying operations for Atlantic Ferry so his new chief was in no doubt that the squadron would be in capable hands.

77 Squadron was based at Leeming, North Yorkshire. It was supposed to be a heavy bomber unit and Don Bennett was therefore disappointed to find it equipped with obsolescent Armstrong Whitworth Whitleys, twin-engined aircraft which could carry a modest bomb load over a radius of only 750 miles. Early in the war Whitleys carried half of all the bombs dropped on Germany and, as he got to know these docile old warbirds, Bennett developed great admiration for their rugged dependability.

There was no lack of courage at 77 Squadron, far from it. If anything was lacking it was expertise and this was to scare the wits out of Don Bennett when he made his first operational trip with a young sergeant pilot at the controls. The raid was over Wilhelmshaven and it got off to a bad start when the pilot rather hastily decided to shut down one engine because he thought it had lost its oil pressure. In fact the engine was fit and well; the oil pressure gauge had failed. Then the bomb aimer was unable to see the target so two runs were made over the area while seemingly every gun in Germany took a shot at the Whitley. On the third run, and by now down to 8000 feet and one engine, Bennett jettisoned the bombs, re-started the 'failed' engine and took command of the badly shot-up Whitley before his sergeant took it into his head to make a fourth run. It had been an education for the new C.O. of 77 Squadron and he was quick to recognise that bombing raids at that phase of the war were too often in the hands of inexperienced youngsters "With the courage of a thousand lions", Bennett once said, but inexperienced nevertheless.

It took only one bombing operation to present Bennett with a clear picture of the situation. Immediately he arranged to fly with a different crew each night, teaching them the finer points of navigation and generally adding a little professionalism where it was needed. He insisted on better night photography so that the results of his squadron's bombing could more accurately be assessed. His Australian training days at Point Cooke were proving useful. He immediately rid his crews of wrongly held beliefs on bomb sight techniques. Previously they had been geared to relatively low level bombing but by 1941 the German guns had encouraged Bomber Command to fly a little higher. However, while on a raid aimed at destroying the Renault works Bennett went in at only 2000 feet. Almost all of Bomber Command took part and it was probably the most successful raid mounted by the RAF up to that stage of the war.

In the early days of the war crews were needlessly lost when damaged aircraft, often flown by inexperienced pilots, crashed while attempting to land. Bennett was appalled at the time being taken by crash crews and those manning the fire tender when these dramas occurred. Often he would arrive at the scene of the crash before those who should have been there first, dealing with fires before they got out of hand and removing the injured while time remained to save lives. The all-pervading amateurism then current in so much of the Royal Air Force was a constant source of irritation to him. There was the case of the *Sharnhorst* and *Gneisenau* two German warships that posed a constant threat to British shipping. They had been holed up in Brest harbour for some months, a weapon of war by their very presence there. The Germans wanted them back in Germany. Their departure from Brest on 12 February 1942 remained undetected by Coastal Command and the two ships might have enjoyed an incident-free cruise up the English Channel but for the sharp eyes of Group Captain Victor Beamish, the famous fighter pilot, who was on patrol along the French coast. In fact the Germans had put up a fighter screen over their two warships and the swarming Luftwaffe could be seen on the British radar screens. What happened thereafter is a sad catalogue of mismanagement, lost opportunities and indecision. Instead of mounting an all-out attack, swamping the fighters and depriving the German navy of two major fighting units, RAF and RN aircraft were sent out in twos and threes, easy meat for the Luftwaffe and no real threat to '*Salmon* and *Gluckstein*' as the two German ships had become known in the British press. Don Bennett repeatedly asked for permission to send in 77 Squadron but he was told to 'stand by'. Stand by he did while a handful of RN Swordfish biplanes were despatched on a suicide mission from which there was little chance of inflicting any material damage on the two big warships — thus it was at a time when amateurs were dictating policy and trying to handle situations demanding the highest standards of professionalism.

Things were not well at Bomber Command. The RAF, even in 1942, operated without the goodwill of the more senior services. The Navy, which based its policy and doctrine on the battleship, was reluctant to believe that either the submarine or aircraft could materially affect its role in the war. The Army had, between wars, deliberately reduced its tank and machine gun content. Much of its thinking was based upon World War I concepts. Indeed, while attending the Army Staff College at Camberley many years before the war an RAF officer by name of Arthur Harris accused his hosts of disliking tanks 'because they did not eat hay — and make a noise like a horse that had eaten too much of it'. The only Army instructor he admired was one Bernard Montgomery (for whom he developed the highest regard in later years) and 'Monty' was viewed with suspicion by the others at the college. The escape to Germany of the *Sharnhorst* and *Gneisenau* was but one example of the serious lack of direction that encumbered Bomber Command during the first few years of the war. From 5 October 1940 it had been under the command of Air Marshal Sir Richard Peirse, KCB, DSO, AFC. In fairness to him he had taken over a force, few in numbers and equipped with aircraft that, even by 1939 standards, could only be described as obsolete. The single-engined Fairey Battle light bomber had been shot out of the skies over France. Blenheim twin-engined light bombers, excellent and advanced as they were in 1937, could only carry a bomb load of 1000 lbs or so and by 1941 they were easy meat for enemy fighters. The slightly larger Handley Page Hampden could lift a respectable 4000 lbs over short distances but when a raid entailed flying to Germany and back the bomb load was halved. The Armstrong Whitworth Whitley would carry about 6000 lbs of bombs along with defensive armament for a distance of 1500 miles but this mainstay of Bomber Command was very slow. Coming into service was the Vickers Wellington, but this highly successful medium bomber, which continued on operational duties with Bomber Command until October 1943, could not carry a large bomb load over long distances. True the first of the new breed of four-engined heavy bombers was due to enter the squadrons but that was for the future.

The biggest weakness had quickly been recognised by Bennett, namely, the inability of bomber crews to find targets at night. The problem had been troubling the Air Ministry since events proved that daylight raids against well defended targets were too costly in terms of lost aircrews and aircraft. During his time with Imperial Airways and later while running Atlantic Ferry, Don Bennet had remained in touch with some of his friends from RAF days when he was at Pembroke Dock and Calshot. Now several of his old colleagues were serving in the Directorate of Bomber Operations at the Air Ministry. Running the department at the time was Air Commodore John Baker and his deputy was Aubrey Ellwood. Another old friend was Wing Commander Cleland and it was he who reminded his seniors of Bennett's shining expertise as a navigator. Perhaps the Master Airman could advise them what to do about target finding.

While in England for a few days rest following an Atlantic delivery Bennett was invited to Air Ministry and asked for his views on the target-finding problem. He answered their questions by posing another. "Could you get into an aircraft on a pitch black night, fly for three or four hours on a compass and an airspeed indicator, find a pinpoint in Central Germany, avoid spoofs and dummies [a reference to German decoys intended to mislead the bomber crews], not be put off by night fighters, flak and searchlights — and guarantee success"? "Of course not" they protested, "We are pilots, not navigators". At this stage of the conversation Don Bennett reminded his friends that they had perhaps twenty years RAF experience whereas the youngsters flying bombers over France and Germany were low on flying hours and hardly dry behind the ears. It was a powerful line of reasoning and what Bennett then proposed was equally logical. A highly trained target-finding force should be set up and this would mark the aiming point with coloured flares. Then the main stream of bombers would carry out the raid. The idea was practical and, even allowing for the lack of radio aids at the time, likely to give good results provided reasonable weather conditions existed at the time of a raid. Now that he was back in the RAF Bennett could appreciate the target-finding problem at first hand. Not unnaturally he asked his friends at the Air Ministry if any action was likely to be taken on his proposals for a target-finding force. Apparently Bomber Command, seemingly well satisfied with its bombing accuracy based upon optimistic crew reports, had turned down the idea but there were rumbles of disbelief from outside the RAF, voices that challenged the recorded bombing successes and claimed that few bombs were reaching the targets. The Directorate of Bomber Operations must have shared these misgivings because Bennett was encouraged to go about his task with Bomber Command and keep in touch with them as their unofficial adviser.

Yes indeed, all was not well at Bomber Command. Enthusiastic crew reports recounted during post-flight debriefings did not accord with photo reconnaissance carried out after the raids. Times were bad for Britain and it was not long before the Army and the Navy were complaining that the Royal Air Force was squandering the nation's resources to little effect. There had been a long history of antagonism between the RAF and the two older services and but for the firm resolve of Sir Hugh Trenchard, generally regarded as the father of the RAF, there would never have been a separate military aviation service in Britain. Nevertheless, the two senior services had grounds for concern. They too needed factories and materials for their fighting men and there was even some talk of splitting Bomber Command so that the Army and the Navy could have their own strategic air arm. The Germans used their Luftwaffe in a supporting role but when the RAF went on to the offensive the wrongness of their own arrangements was forceably brought home to the German High Command.

In the face of mounting concern about bombing inaccuracies a committee was set up under the chairmanship of an able civil servant named D. M. Butt. He and his colleagues studied many night photographs taken during raids that occurred throughout June and July 1941. Their findings, published on 18 August that year, were, to say the least, alarming. In essence the Butt Report, as it become known, claimed that of the aircraft that attacked the target only one in three bombed within five miles of the aiming point. Over Germany the figures were one in four while over the Ruhr, a difficult area permanently obscured by industrial haze, the proportion was only one bomber in ten. As the weather conditions became more difficult (thick cloud, dense haze etc.) a mere one crew in fifteen got within five miles of the target — and over Europe the weather was more often bad than good. Few bombs were reaching the target, others were scattered 10 — 20 — 30 — 40 and even 50 miles away.

Morale sank at Bomber Command when the findings of the Butt Report became known. Aircrews naturally felt they were being sacrificed to no purpose. The command was suffering from the combined effects of unsuitable aircraft, lack of radio aids and inappropriate training for the task in hand. To make matters worse, the best and most experienced crews were often moved out of the squadrons and posted to different commands. The Butt Report provided abundant evidence in support of Bennett's contention that a specially trained target-finding force was urgently required yet the months went by and little was done to change the pattern of things. Air Chief Marshal Sir Richard Pierse was at first unable to accept the facts of the report but the truth had to be faced. It was time for radical changes. On 23 February 1942 Air Chief Marshal Sir Arthur T. Harris became C-in-C Bomber Command. He was clear-thinking, tough and resourceful, and he had a talent for making people of conflicting temperaments work together. In one of his few public statements, on his appointment he said of the Germans "They have sown the wind — and they shall reap the whirlwind". Whether or not Hitler and his followers took heed of these words is difficult to say. But they would have good cause to reflect on them in the months and years to come.

Much ill-informed nonsense has been written since the war about Sir Arthur Harris's successful bomber operations. So-called liberal minds have accused him of slaughtering German civilians and failing to achieve any tangible results from the misery created by Bomber Command. Self-appointed experts of air and military strategy, few of them with more than a passing knowledge of the events that made it necessary for Britain to bomb Nazi Germany or an understanding of what was in store for the UK and the rest of the world had the Third Reich prevailed, would have us believe that Harris alone decided to destroy civil targets and that Bomber Command failed to have any material effect on the German war effort. In the first place Harris, even in his capacity as Commander in Chief, was responsible to higher authority. And on 14 February, 1942 the Air Ministry issued directive S46368/D.C.A.S. which stated in clear terms that Bomber Command was " — to focus attacks on the morale of the enemy civil population and, in particular, of the industrial workers".

A further directive dated 21 January 1943 charged him with the task of destroying four large cities in the Ruhr, centre of German heavy industry, and severely damaging another 14 industrial cities. Earlier, in fact on 23 September 1941, an Air Staff paper had defined Bomber Command's task in these words:-
    "the ultimate aim of the attack on a town area is to break the

morale of the population which occupies it. To ensure this, we must achieve two things; first we must make the town physically uninhabitable and, secondly, we must make the people conscious of constant personal danger. The immediate aim is therefore twofold, namely, to produce (i) destruction, and (ii) the fear of death".

Clearly Harris had been given his instructions although he was in full agreement with the general policy of the War Council. The equally unfounded claim that, for all its terrible destruction Bomber Command had little effect on the course of the war, will be dismantled in the pages that follow.

The appointment of his old chief of pre-war flying boat days as C-in-C Bomber Command was heartening news for Don Bennett who greatly admired Harris.

"He had been my CO at Pembroke Dock when I was in 210 Squadron — and there I learned that he was full of fire and dash, was not easily baulked and was also remarkably intelligent without trying to show it. He was, I knew, a *real* man and my hopes for the bomber offensive and its ultimate destruction of Germany were revitalised."

Those were Don Bennett's recollections of his feelings when Arthur Harris took over Bomber Command. Looking back on his impressions of the great man he had this to add 42 years later:-

"He was a little overweight but his genial personality gave an impression of one younger than Harris. He was very often right, he could be very rude and his outspoken ways made him unpopular with the Army and the Navy".

Bennett regards this as a compliment to Harris. When Harris took over the situation at Bomber Command was bleak indeed. Out of a miserable total of 378 serviceable aircraft, some of them crewed by part-trained personnel, only 69 were heavies; the planned re-equipment of bomber squadrons with large, four-engined aircraft had barely started. The new C-in-C was quick to recognise the urgent need for more aircraft, better trained crews, improved tactics and effective radio navigation aids. The essential role of radio aids had long been recognised and in November 1940 Bomber Command was asking for some form of radar which would enable it to locate targets when the ground was obscured by fog or low cloud. It was not until early 1943 that the first of the 'black boxes' became generally available to bomber squadrons although a few aircraft were fitted with the device by the end of February 1942. In fact it was used for the first time against Essen on the night of 8 March that year.

The equipment was called GEE. It consisted of a ground based 'master' transmitter and additional 'slave' stations. These transmitters radiated synchronised pulse signals which were received in the aircraft by equipment capable of measuring time differences between master and slave stations to an accuracy of micro seconds. These measurements varied according to the aircraft's distance from the GEE transmitters. The navigator adjusted controls on his GEE box until the correct image appeared on a small cathode ray tube. Readings thus obtained for each master-slave pair were then referred to purpose-designed GEE charts overprinted with a lattice pattern representing the radiation from the 'master' and 'slave' stations. Each line was numbered and where they crossed on the map represented the aircraft's position. Range was limited to 300 — 350 miles.

Early enthusiasm for GEE was soon tempered by the realisation that, at longer ranges, it was not accurate enough to enable precision target location. Although the RAF tried to create the impression that accurate radio beams were being used, the Germans, with characteristic resourcefulness, got wind of the new radio aid and started jamming its signals. By August 1942 even before GEE had become standard equipment in all bomber aircraft, it ceased to give navigational guidance once the north coast of Europe was crossed. However, anti-jamming devices were developed and, to some extent, this restored its effectiveness. But many crews regarded GEE as no more than a 'get-you-started' and a 'get-you-home' aid. Nevertheless, GEE was accurate enough to ensure that at least 50 per cent of all bombs would fall on a large town, even when it was obscured by cloud. It also enabled the RAF bombers to operate more frequently than before since they were less affected by the weather. This factor alone was calculated to have increased the effectiveness of Harris's puny force of 300 bombers by a factor of seven. However, the destruction of vital targets, such as the Krupps industrial complex in the Ruhr, remained an unsolved problem for the simple reason that the average bomber crew had not the skill to navigate with sufficient accuracy, even with the aid of GEE. Bennett's solution was on the table, yet it continued to be rejected although, from time to time, he would remind his Air Ministry friends of the situation.

In the spring of 1942 events were temporarily to engage the ever-active mind of Don Bennett on a matter other than his proposed target-finding force. The long awaited four-engined heavy bombers were slowly being issued to the squadrons, first the towering Short Stirling with its enormously long, double-jointed undercarriage (it was the first four-engined bomber to enter RAF service since the mammoth Handley Page V/1500 biplanes of 1919). Soon afterwards came the Handley Page Halifax and these aircraft could carry more than three times the war load of the medium bombers. Bennett was posted to RAF Leeming there to command No. 10 Squadron which flew the Halifax. Not long after his arrival a special assignment came his way. The German battleship *Tirpitz* was anchored at Aasfjord near Trondheim in Norway. He was to destroy it.

An audacious plan had been devised by the British Royal Navy. The idea was that spherical mines would be dropped by 10 Squadron. These would roll down the adjacent banks of the fjord, into the sea and then under the great battleship where depth fuses would detonate the mines with appropriate and spectacular results. To create a diversion while Bennett and his team flew at a few hundred feet, two other Halifax squadrons would bomb at high level. It was hoped that they would draw off fire from those coming in low.

As Bennett's aircraft crossed the Norwegian coast all hell broke loose, they were hit by ground fire and the rear gunner was wounded. Other German naval units opened fire as they approached the *Tirpitz* and while descending to the pre-arranged 200-foot bombing level the right hand wing caught fire, its fuel tank blazing away in spectacular manner. The battleship was covered in camouflage and that made its location difficult. It later transpired that this was known to Naval Intelligence who had thought fit to keep the information to themselves; inter-service rivalry could still rear its ugly head, even in times of war.

On his first pass over the *Tirpitz* Don Bennett caught a fleeting glimpse of the battleship's superstructure but by then it was pointless to release the mines; they would have landed several hundred yards past the target. He turned and made a second run while the fire intensified. By now the starboard undercarriage leg had decided to lower itself and the flaps on the burning wing were partly depressed. The future for that Halifax and its crew was not looking good during those hectic moments so Bennett estimated as best he could the position of the *Tirpitz*, released the mines and turned his stricken bomber towards neutral Sweden. In true British war film tradition, the voice of a crew member came up on the intercom. "Cheerio chaps — this is it — we've had it". To which Bennett retorted "Shut up and make ready to bale out. There is no danger if you keep your heads". Now clearly this was a masterpiece of understatement, having regard to the facts of the situation, but Bennett's handling of it was a prime example of first class leadership under trying conditions.

Ahead was a 3000-foot range of mountains which the Halifax had no intention of clearing on half a wing so the order was given "Abandon aircraft; jump, jump". It was at this stage that Bennett realised he was at the controls of a burning aircraft, in a harness only. The all essential parachute which attached to this webbing was in its rack behind the cockpit. This was not time to be without a parachute and he was debating with himself the possibility of leaving his seat and finding the 'chute at a time when the Halifax was becoming unmanageable when Flight Sergeant Colgan his flight engineer appeared. He was a brave man that Flight Sergeant. Instead of baling out when told he first located his commander's parachute, helped him clip it to the harness, then crawled to the rear turret and evacuated the wounded tail gunner. They got out of the aircraft together. Seconds later, as the starboard wing finally succumbed to the blazing heat of a petrol fire and folded back, Don Bennett abandoned his Halifax. By now it had descended below the minimum level for safe use of a parachute. He pulled the ripcord and hit the snow as the canopy fully opened. Had there been one further second delay in leaving that aircraft this biography of D. C. T. Bennett would have ended here.

What are one's first reaction in a situation of this kind? Events move quickly, there are impression of gunfire, noise, the black sky, a difficult-to-fly bomber and the anxiety of a major fire in one wing. Fire at any time can be dreadful. In an aeroplane it takes on a new dimension of fearfulness. When the wing folded there was no question of staying with the Halifax. At that point it was transformed from a flying machine to a complex of uncontrolled metal, tumbling random fashion as it hurtled earthwards in the black night. The arrival in the snow, seconds after pulling the ripcord was just another frantic event which, on top of all others, was difficult to take in. Bennett's first reaction was concern for his wife Ly and her shock at being told he was missing.

Some thirty minutes later he ran into another figure in the dark and fearing it might be a German soldier Bennett drew his revolver. The man put up his arms and then Bennett recognised that it was his wireless operator, Sergeant Forbes. Together they were to walk many miles across the snow and ice of Norway. There were icy streams to cross (which destroyed the trails and confused the German tracker dogs), mountains to climb and snow to make the going harder. Exhaustion built up to the point where houses could be seen where none existed.

RAF aircrew were issued with an escape kit consisting of a silk handkerchief which was a map of the operating area, a small compass, a tin of Horlicks tables and some barley sugars. There was also a small rubber bag which could be used for carrying water. The wireless operator was wearing his sheepskin lined leather flying jacket, Bennett was not warmly clad and the going was particularly tough for him. Their flying boots would fill with water while crossing streams and it was not long before this froze to add to the discomfort.

The map showed a railway line and this they located, striking off towards a little town, on the way by-passing a German sentry guarding a bridge. By now their condition was critical and time had come to take chances. It was a case of risk being caught or face death from exposure. They knocked on the door of an isolated house. A terrified young girl answered soon to be joined by her parents. The family stared at the exhausted pair, refusing to respond to their obvious appeals for food. At that stage Bennett turned to Forbes and said "Get ready to run. I don't like the look of this". Immediately the Norwegians answered in English and invited them in. They had suspected them of being Germans intent on causing trouble for them. That night a young Norwegian led them to the Swedish border, they staggered down a snow-covered slope and made for a brightly lit building where young couples were dancing. After the initial shock of seeing two scruffy RAF aircrew on their doorstep Bennett and Forbes were invited in, wined and dined and generally treated as celebrities — 72 hours after being shot down!

Bennett formed the impression that during this period of the war the Swedish Army was not only pro-German but anti-British while the Swedish Air Force supported the RAF and the Allies. A Captain Skoogk of the Swedish Army arrived and courteously announced that Bennett and Forbes were under arrest. Next day he sent a coded telegram to Ly Bennett at Leeming telling her that Wing Commander Bennett was alive and well in Sweden. The actual wording was "Love Captain Skoog" ('love' being the Bennett's code for 'arrived' which they had derived during Imperial Airways days). The events that followed were pure farce. Ly Bennett advised RAF Leeming who in turn told the Air Ministry. That worthy establishment then sent a telegram to Ly Bennett which said " — from an unreliable source it is believed that Wing Commander Bennett is alive".

It was while attending the local public baths that Bennett encountered a menswear shop where he and Forbes kitted themselves out somewhat lavishly, sending the bill to the British Embassy in Stockholm. Back at the internment camp Flight Sergeant Colgan (the flight engineer who had saved Bennett's life) and Sergeant Walmsley, the second pilot, had meanwhile arrived in reasonably good condition. In fact of the seven crew in Halifax W1041 all survived although the wounded tail gunner and two others were captured by the Germans.

Internment camp, however friendly it may be, did not suit Don Bennett at all. He contacted the British Embassy and made the point that as an escaped prisoner of war he and his crew had lost their belligerent status and should therefore not be interned. Response from the Embassy was singularly unhelpful. Little changes at the British Foreign Office but the Embassy staff was soon to learn what kind of a man they were dealing with when they were confronted by the young Wing Commander. Education was close at hand when through the kind endeavours of two Australian ladies, one of them married to a Swede, Bennett was let loose on parole. He descended on the British Embassy to find that little was being done to get him repatriated. To keep him quiet they arranged a meeting with Count Bernadotte, at the time Swedish Foreign Minister. Bennett let it be known that, if necessary he would take the Count to court unless he was allowed home. They extended his stay in Stockholm while these unusual and perhaps unprecedented demands were considered. The wires must have been burning between Stockholm and London because it was not long before he was released. And at that stage the Embassy staff gave up the fight and actually became helpful. The Naval Attaché even produced information on the *Tirpitz* that had been sent to London which, had it been made available to Bomber Command before the raid, might well have resulted in a very different outcome.

For some considerable time the British Ambassador in Stockholm had tried without success to obtain a flight back to London and he was rather less than enchanted when a Lockheed 14 complete with Norwegian pilot was provided for the young Wing Commander. It flew him to England in clear weather and through airspace that was under the complete control of the Germans. It was a case of audacious action taking the enemy by surprise.

From being shot down in Halifax W1041 to arriving back in England spanned a period of exactly one month. For his efforts Don Bennett was awarded the DSO. It had always been the practice not to allow escaping officers to resume operational duties. However, while evading the Germans no-one had been killed and they gave him back his command of 10 Squadron on the very day that Air Chief Marshal Sir Arthur Harris mounted his first 1000 bomber raid. Soon afterwards 10 Squadron was moved to the Middle East for operations against the Italian Navy. One hour before leaving England Bennett received an urgent message. He was to report immediately to 'Bomber' Harris. The Italian Navy would be spared the professional attention of Donald Clifford Tyndall Bennett. The Gods of War had more important things for him to do.

Chapter 7
Enter the Pathfinders

It is now necessary to focus attention away from Donald Bennett. He was not alone in recognising the need for a highly trained target-finding force. The idea had been championed for some time by Sydney Bufton, one of three brothers to serve as pilots in the RAF. Early in the war he had commanded a squadron of Fairey Battle single-engined light bombers. When the Germans broke through France he did not fly back to England until after the Dunkirk evacuation. Bufton commanded 10 Squadron between July 1940 and April 1941 (later Don Bennett was C/O of this squadron) and it was while flying Whitleys on operation duties that the true problems of target location at night were revealed. Yet time and time again some crews seemed able to find the aiming point. Why? What was special about these pilots, navigators, bomb aimers and wireless operator/air gunners? By the autumn of 1940 Bufton had formulated ideas for a specialist target-finding force and he was pressing for suitable flares with barometric fuses which ensured illumination at the correct height above the ground. The idea was to turn night into day by dropping clusters of flares over the target area, thus enabling the bomb aimer to visually identify the aiming point. But often the crews would complain of being blinded by the direct glare from these pyrotechnics and, on Bufton's suggestion, hoods were attached to the flare cases. In effect these shielded the bomber crews from direct glare. Like Don Bennett, he recognised the importance of having good navigators and bomb aimers — without them the best of pilots would be unable to find targets in the dark. Indeed Bennett had offered similar advice to the Air Ministry when, at the invitation of Wing Commander Ralph Cleland (Bomber Ops.), he discussed the problem with him towards the end of 1940.

Bufton devised a system which in many respects anticipated

the techniques that were later to effect dramatic improvement in bombing accuracy. The system was simple and logical. The first crews to identify the target with certainty would fire Very lights in a pre-arranged colour code. The target would be illuminated by a number of hooded flares and then the bombs would be dropped. It was found possible to carry 36 bundles of flares in a Wellington and 104 in the much bigger Stirling, each bundle consisting of three flares. On 1 November 1941 Group Captain Bufton was posted to Bomber Operations at the Air Ministry. By then he had formed the first Halifax squadron (No. 76) and commanded a Canadian Bomber station at Pocklington. His work on improved flares and target location had not gone unnoticed. Certainly the views of Syd Bufton were respected by his chief, Air Commodore John Baker. He was invited to write a paper outlining his proposals for a specialist target-finding force. At the time Air Vice-Marshal Jack Baldwin was acting head of Bomber Command pending the arrival of Harris and although he expressed interest in the ideas put forward by Bufton it was thought best to take no action until the new C-in-C had arrived. However Bufton's theories were put to the test in one of the most successful raids carried out by Bomber Command up to that stage of the war.

On 3 March 1942 an attack using Bufton's method was mounted against the giant Renault works at Bioncore, Paris. The factory was saturated with flares which could be seen from the French coast and a high concentration of bombs found the target as a result. By way of contrast, five nights later, on the evening of 8 March, GEE was used for the first time, the target was Essen and the old method of using flares in penny numbers, dropping them singly one every five miles, failed to provide a suitable concentration of light. The method used at Essen was known as the *Shaker* technique. It had been devised by Bomber Command. And it was a failure.

Encouraged by the success of the Renault raid Bomber Operations urged Bufton to develop his ideas. He was, of course, not alone in putting forward schemes for revolutionising bomber techniques. Churchill received letters by the score suggesting aerial mine fields, marker bombs and all manner of devices, some of them certain to prove more lethal to the RAF than the enemy. One weapon took the form of a drainpipe-like structure with a spiked nose. It would drop from an aircraft, impale itself into the ground and then burn like a giant Roman Candle. Churchill would forward these letters to Lord Cherwell, his scientific adviser, and he in turn sent them to the Directorate of Bomber Operations for comment.

One fact was emerging; incendiary bombs were proving more effective than had been anticipated. Ton for ton, they caused more damage than high explosive bombs. In fact Wing Commander Arthur Morley, a man of varied experience who was an expert on target selection (taking into account the effect its destruction would have on the German economy) devoted much of his time to selling the value of incendiaries to the squadrons. Now that the importance of target marking was becoming recognised Morley felt certain that the answer lay in mass dropping of coloured incendiaries. He discussed his views with Bufton, drawing patterns of how the incendiaries should land. Some of these were several hundred yards wide and perhaps half a mile long. The effect would be like diamonds seen against a black velvet cloth, clear, unmistakable, thus presenting an ideal aiming point. Most of the incendiary bombs currently in use were difficult to aim with accuracy because their ballistic properties were so poor. However, the proposed markers would have to be dropped with precision if they were to be of any value to the main bomber force and, even at that stage, it was recognised that a variety of different colours would be required.

The Ministry of Aircraft Production was already working on a 250 lb bomb containing three rows of 20 incendiaries. The outer case was of good ballistic shape and a barometric fuse could be set to eject the incendiaries at the required height above ground level. The plan was to develop this idea and substitute incendiaries for pyrotechnic candles of whatever colour was required. Each layer of candles, which burned for about three and a half minutes, could be a different colour. So the marker might burn green, then yellow and then red (or whatever combination of colours was required). In that way the Germans would find it difficult to mount convincing decoys aimed at misleading the main bomber force. Trials of the new markers were conducted at Boscombe Down on 30 June. They were an instant success — you could see them for 40 miles. Suitable Target Indicators had thus arrived six months before the RAF had a specialist force with the skill to drop them in the right places.

Since taking over as C in C Bomber Command Air Chief Marshal Sir Arthur Harris had of necessity to devote much of his time to assessing the problems of his inadequate force. He quickly recognised the need for some kind of target-finding force but his ideas were very different to those of Don Bennett or Sydney Bufton. Nevertheless, on 16 March, only a matter of weeks after assuming command, Harris agreed to Bufton presenting his views at a meeting of Bomber Command Group Commanders. Bufton was a young Group Captain about to be surrounded by Air Vice-Marshals led by their formidable chief so John Baker, head of Bomber Operations, came along to give moral support. Before the meeting there was an informal talk in Harris's office during which the Commander in Chief made clear his total opposition to the idea of a *Corps d'Elite*. Bufton assured Harris that this was not the intention; the objective was to find the targets and mark them with Target Indicators recently developed for the purpose. His idea was to take 40 pilots, one from each other squadron, and form a six-squadron target-finding-force which would be trained to the highest standards. At that point it would become self-generating. Harris warned that if he were to take good flight commanders out of their squadrons they would lose their chances of promotion. As firmly as he could Bufton retorted "Sir, we will never win the war that way — these chaps don't know whether they are going to be alive tomorrow and they couldn't care less about promotion. All they want is to do a really good job". Recalling the occasion forty-two years later Bufton, by then a retired Air Vice-Marshal, said:-

"At that stage we went to lunch with Bert in a bit of a huff [Harris had collected the name Bert from a song the like of which is not usually performed in respectable company]. We then assembled and Bert said — "Well gentlemen, I've called you here to discuss this very emotive subject of a target-finding force. I was almost assaulted in my office this morning and there is no need for me to tell you that I am totally opposed to it. Nevertheless, I would like to give you all an opportunity to express your own views on it."

None of the Group Commanders present had flown on operations; apart from Bufton the only other officer at the meeting with first hand operational experience was the relatively junior one who took the minutes. All the Group Commanders opposed the idea of a special force so it was a disappointed John Baker and Sydney Bufton who returned to Air Ministry.

The following morning Bufton was parking his car in King Charles Street alongside the Air Ministry when Harris arrived in his Bentley. Bufton saluted and stood aside. As he entered the building Harris said "Good morning Bufton. What are you going to do to me today?" To which Bufton replied, "I wasn't going to do anything, Sir". Apparently Harris was visiting Portal, the Chief of Air Staff and he invited Bufton to walk upstairs with him so that they could talk. Despite his total opposition to the specialist force Harris invited Bufton to write privately if he had any ideas about future bombing techniques.

The generous attitude adopted by Arthur Harris was typical of the great man and Sydney Bufton was quick to take up the invitation. Without delay he got together his like-minded colleagues and they compiled a long letter which was sent to Harris on 17 March 1942. It contained more than 2000 words typed on three foolscap pages of closely reasoned arguments in favour of a target-finding force. In it Bufton said that his ideas, which were based on his own operational experience and that of others, had been matured over a long period. He mentioned the importance of good flares for finding the aiming point and the need to mark it with distinctive target indicators. He expressed the view that Squadron and Group Commanders were too near the woods to see the trees and, in consequence, unable fully to comprehend the problem facing bomber crews trying to locate a target at night, often in poor weather. The letter made a case for allowing six above average squadrons to work in close liaison. As a team they would devise new target-finding techniques and thus generate a 'great force of enthusiasm'. The objection relating to possible effects on promotion was discounted as of little importance and such resentment as may result from creaming-off the best squadrons was a non-recurring problem; the target-finding force would develop its own techniques and henceforth train new crews as they entered from the Operational Training Units. In any case:-

"The ability to find and actually to see their target would be an inspiration to the rest of the Bomber Force and this in itself would more than outweigh any drop in efficiency and morale which might result from the removal of one good crew from each squadron".

In his letter Bufton stressed the urgent need for an improvement in Bomber Command's performance to counter political and other forces intent on its disruption. Documents supporting these arguments accompanied Bufton's letter.

On 17 April Air Marshal Harris replied to the effect that although he had "a fairly open mind on the subject of the Target-Finding Force" he was not convinced by the arguments put forward. He said that his Group Commanders were against the idea and so were senior members of his headquarters staff. He also claimed that the majority of the Station Commanders were not in favour of Bufton's proposals. He added " — I am not prepared to accept all the very serious disadvantages of a *Corps d'Elite* in order to secure possibly some improvement on methods which are already proving reasonably satisfactory and certainly very costly to the enemy". Harris proposed that each group should in future develop its own target-finding methods and the squadrons with the best results would be designated Target-Finding Force for the ensuing month.

The value of competition as a means of attaining the best results cannot be denied. But there were compelling arguments in favour of having a permanent force specially trained and equipped for the target-finding task. Coloured Target Indicators (TIs) accurately positioned in the light of many flares would certainly enable the bomber force to drop most of its bombs in the right place. But this was only possible when the ground could be seen. Low cloud, fog or industrial haze, all of them the rule rather than the exception in Northern Europe, totally disrupted the procedure and under such conditions location of the target demanded the use of radio aids of a kind more accurate than any currently available. Such 'black boxes' were under development. They were very much more accurate than GEE, so much so that eventually Target Indicators could be placed within fifty or so yards of the aiming point, even when the area was unseen. More will be said later about these remarkable radio aids but at this point in the story it should be explained that the equipment could only handle one aircraft every ten minutes or so. Surely it made sense to entrust the use of this new, top secret and very accurate target-finding equipment to one specialist unit. In this belief Bufton and Bennett were completely in accord although the two men had reached their conclusions entirely independently.

Harris was a man of vision and great intelligence. He had prophesied the fall of France and that the British forces would be thrown out of Europe. Although most of the war leaders regarded a German invasion of Britain as almost certain he never felt there was the slightest chance of this happening. He was equally certain that the only way Britain could bring pressure to bear on Germany was by bombing its industrial towns and major military targets with an intensity never before attempted by any air force. This he was determined to do in furtherance of the policy laid down for him. He was in no doubt about the difficulties of target location at night but although acknowledging the need for new techniques he firmly opposed any steps that entailed "creaming-off the best crews of all the Groups in order to form a *Corps d'Elite*". Clearly, Syd Bufton would not find it easy to change the mind of a strong character like Arthur Harris.

A paper setting out his case for a target-finding force was circulated to bomber pilots of experience. It invited their comments and encouraged replies in the frankest terms. These were sent to Air Marshal Harris who courteously rejected the proposals yet again. In the exchange of correspondence that followed Bufton pushed his views as strongly as he could. He was, after all, a Group Captain dealing with an Air Marshal. Somehow Harris go hold of the idea that Bufton was trying to gain the support of an MP but this he refuted in his letter to Harris of 8 May. He also drew attention to the continuing inaccuracy of Bomber Command and of a recent raid on Rostock he was able to claim "78% of our effort, as far as aim was concerned, was wasted. Correct tactics could have more than quadrupled the effect of this raid". He also commented on other raids, all of them made in good weather — all resulting in a very small proportion of the bombs actually dropping within the target area. Pushing his luck to the limit Bufton said there appeared to be "a conflict of ideas between the older officers of much general experience and the ever growing body of younger ones who have been actively engaged in operations".

Matters came to a head in the most unexpected circumstances. Air Commodore Baker was away and, as Deputy Director, Bufton was occupying his office. At about 10 am the door quietly opened and a head came around. It was Air Marshal Sir Wilfred Freeman, Vice-Chief of Air Staff. "Good morning Bufton, are you having any problems?" He acquainted the Deputy CAS of his Target-Finding Force saga and in response to a request for papers handed over the file. An hour later Bufton was sent for. "I have read all the correspondence" he was told by Freeman. "Leave it to me — I will show it to the CAS". The file must have impressed Air Chief Marshal Sir Charles (later Lord) Portal because the following Monday he sent for Bufton, expressed his firm support for the idea of a target-finding force and asked him to list some outline proposals, giving an order of battle and recommending who should command the force. Plans were drawn up for a six squadron force to be commanded by Air Vice-Marshal Basil Embry, a resourceful officer who led a light bomber force specialising in low level attacks. He had been shot down on one of these raids but managed to escape back to

England. Senior Air Staff Officer (SASO) was to be Don Bennett whose technical excellence and flying skill were well known to Bufton.

When Harris was told by Portal that he must set up a Target-Finding Force on the lines proposed by Bufton and his colleagues he is alleged to have said "Over my dead body". The Chief of Air Staff politely advised him to go away and think about the order he had just received, and his reply. Next morning Harris saw Portal and agreed to set up the new force but he felt that it had been imposed on him and it rankled to his last days. He wrote to the Prime Minister complaining that he had been " — overborne by the CAS and the Air Staff". In his end of war *Despatch on War Operations*, a masterly volume of facts, graphs and figures compiled by Harris, he said of these events:-

"The Air Ministry, however, insisted on the formation of a separate Pathfinder Force as a separate Group — yet another occasion when a Commander in the field was overruled at the dictation of junior staff officers at the Air Ministry".

Of course this was not strictly correct because in the end it was Portal who insisted on the target-finding force. But why did Bufton risk the displeasure of a C-in-C by pressing for something that Harris mistrusted and disliked? There were personal reasons. First, he had almost lost his life taking part in bombing raids that had little chance of success. Then his younger brother John had been killed in a Hampden during November 1940 and at one time the youngest of the family, Harold (Hal) Bufton was missing presumed killed, although he escaped through Spain and later played a vital role in the so-called 'secret war'. The impact of early bombing operations on his family, coupled with his own experiences, had impelled him to recognise the need for a specialist force, the nature of which closely resembled proposals put forward by Don Bennett before he had re-joined the RAF. Surprisingly these proposals, made by Bennett during his various private visits to the Air Ministry, were never discussed with Bufton.

In his 92nd year, and by then Marshal of the Royal Air Force Sir Arthur Harris, he was asked if he remembered Sydney Bufton. With his typical, dry humour Sir Arthur replied, "Yes, I do indeed. Bufton wanted to run Bomber Command while I took the responsibility. He was a good fellow except that as a staff officer at the Air Ministry you must not imagine you are also the commander".

One must, to some extent, sympathise with Harris. He had

barely taken over Bomber Command before the Air Ministry was pressing him to accept an idea that conflicted with his views and those of his group commanders. However, a reluctant Harris may have bowed to the wishes of his Chief of Air Staff but he was determined to set up the new force on his own terms and in his own way.

Basil Embry would not be the commander — he had someone else in mind. Thus it was that Don Bennett, due to take his squadron to the Middle East within the hour, was summoned to HQ Bomber Command. There, Harris spoke frankly but without bitterness. He made no bones about having been ordered to set up the new force. While totally against the idea he promised Bennett that he would do everything possible to support him. He was promoting Bennett to Acting Group Captain, but since the appointment demanded someone of more senior rank he would command it in the name of the C-in-C and operate as a Staff Officer of H.Q. Bomber Command. Harris refused to accept the title 'Target-Finding Force'. Instead he would call it 'Pathfinder Force' (which rolls nicely off the tongue even if it does not accurately describe the function of the force). And having firmly opposed the setting up of a *Corps d'Elite* he immediately took all steps likely to ensure it would become just that. He devised the famous Pathfinder badge which was to become a cherished emblem to those who served in the force and orders were given to promote all aircrew serving in the new squadron. Thus a Sergeant would become a Flight Sergeant, a Flight Lieutenant got his 'scraper' and was a Squadron Leader. Squadron Commanders in the heavy bomber units were mostly upgraded from Wing Commander to Group Captain. Forty years later Bennett described Harris as "blunt, honest and to the point as always" during the interview but some of his proposals were alarming. For example, Pathfinder crews would be expected to complete a tour of 60 operations instead of the usual 30 although "physical or nervous failure after he had completed a total of 30 sorties will not be regarded as lack of moral fibre".

The stage was set. A perceptive Sydney Bufton had persuaded the Chief of Air Staff to adop a new line of thinking in bombing tactics. He in turn had forced a reluctant C-in-C Bomber Command to set up the Pathfinders and this tough, resourceful Air Marshal then had the genius to pick the best possible commander. Donald Clifford Tyndall Bennett of Toowoomba was about to embark on the most important phase of his varied and hectic career.

Chapter 8
Setting up shop

Pathfinder Force started life with clipped wings. Harris devised a somewhat involved command structure which placed Don Bennett in day-to-day charge but at the mercy of Group Commanders who had consistently opposed the new force. Chain of command followed one of those complex administrative arrangements that is a part of the British heritage. It worked this way:-

1. Pathfinder Force personnel were commanded by Group Captain D. C. T. Bennett.

2. Pathfinder squadrons were lodger units on other stations where the permanent staff was commanded by Air Vice-Marshal J. E. A. Baldwin, A.O.C. of 3 Group.

3. Orders to Pathfinder Force were routed through 3 Group.

4. When aircraft and personnel were lost in action Bennett had to obtain replacements from the original source — the Group that had been 'robbed' in the first place and which, in consequence, were hostile to Pathfinder Force.

Don Bennett was appointed to the new job on 5 July 1942 and, having enlisted the help of the Met. Office in an effort to find an airfield with a good weather record, he set up shop at RAF station Wyton. His modest headquarters staff consisted of Wing Commander Witt, Squadron Leader Angus Anderson and Flying Officer 'Barny' Barnicot. Corporal Ralph, a WAAF who became known as 'Sunshine' acted as Bennett's secretary.

Wyton had Graveley as a satellite airfield and Bennett also used Oakington with its satellite, Warboys. Although Harris, acting rather harshly, had originally ordered that Pathfinder crews would fly tours of 60 (in the event reduced to 45) instead of the usual 30 operations, against much opposition from the

Treasury he pressed through with his plans for promoting aircrews by one rank. The Pathfinder badge, a bronze bird in flight worn under the usual aircrew wings, at first caused trouble within the RAF. Pathfinder crews were often stopped and placed on a charge for being improperly dressed until a blast from Harris made the position clear and reminded all concerned that it had been approved by the King. That badge was no automatic handout; it had to be earned. The original Pathfinder Force was formed around 156, 7, 35 and 83 squadrons which had been taken from Groups 1, 3, 4 and 5 respectively. There was also 109 Squadron from the Wireless Intelligence Development Unit.

While Pathfinder Force was being formed Bennett spent much of his time at the Telecommunications Research Establishment (T.R.E.) based in Great Malvern (now known as the R.S.R.E.). They were developing a revolutionary new bombing aid, a downward-scanning radar which painted a picture of the ground below. It depended upon centimetre wavelengths and these were made possible by the Magnetron, a device invented by T. Randall and H. A. H. Boot. Phillip Dee and Bernard Lovell (later of radio telescope fame) worked on the project which was originally given the code name T.F. (Town Finding). Professor Lindemann (later Lord Cherwell) recognising that this could give the game away and warn the Germans in advance of the new aid, had the name changed to H2S which some claim was an ingenious abbreviation of Home Sweet Home. A more forthright version of how the name was chosen is that when the illustrious professor was shown the new radio aid in crude form he said "I think it stinks". From then on it was known as H2S. Bennett spent six weeks at Defford where the early H2S trials were based. Everyone was saying it would take 10 years to develop the aid but in Bennett they had a pilot who could speak the language of the back room boys — the scientists who devised so many remarkable radio and radar devices during the war years.

At 2 a.m. one morning Bennett was in the test aircraft when an image came up on the little H2S screen. Excitedly he shouted "I can see Gloucester — the Severn Estuary is as clear as a bell — and there is Cheltenham!"

At Defford Bennett was dismayed to find that the ground crews had a passion for pulling apart the development aircraft for no good reason — it was not his way of doing things at all. If they were to make any real progress it would be necessary to fly day and night so he brought in his own experienced maintenance crew from 4 Group. H2S was then developed to a reasonable standard in a matter of weeks. Prior to the arrival of Bennett the H2S programme almost came to a halt when V9977, the Halifax being used for development flying, crashed killing the crew and five of the small team of civilian technicians who were working on the project. However, by 31 December 1942, 24 Halifax and 24 Stirling bombers had been fitted with the as yet unreliable equipment.

Early versions of H2S needed expert eyes to interpret what was below the aircraft. It could indicate a coastline and small towns but a large city swamped the screen with blurred echoes. Later equipment had much improved definition but at one time TRE was criticising Harris and Bennett for not using it as a blind bombing aid, not realising that all crews did not possess the skill to decipher its echoes accurately enough. Harris responded by sending a blunt message to the Air Ministry. "Tell TRE to mind their own bloody business."

Practically without exception wherever he went within Bomber Command Don Bennett met hostility from the Group Commanders. They resented losing some of their best crews and even ordered many of them not to volunteer for the new Pathfinder Force. But at least he did have one friend, Air Vice-Marshal C. R. (Roddy) Carr, AOC 4 Group. Don Bennett had served under him and in the months and years to come the older man, who admired young Bennett, could be relied upon to give his support.

Officially Pathfinder Force was formed on 15 August 1942. Harris allowed no time for training and but for bad weather which cancelled all operations for several nights it would have led a bombing assignment that very evening. In the event it took part in a bombing raid on Flensburg on the night of 18/19 August. Many have expressed the view that Harris was deliberately trying to discredit the new force; he wanted it to fail so that he could tell the Air Ministry "You see — I told you so." Bennett does not subscribe to this opinion; much as he would have liked time to train and develop a cohesive force he could understand Arthur Harris's press-on spirit, get the show on the road and on no account waste crews, fuel and time which were vital to the war effort. Such attitudes were most admired by Bennett.

The Flensburg raid entailed marking a submarine base. There were no radar or other navaids available to the Pathfinders, just a lot of experience, above average skills and a load of parachute flares. The raid was blighted by unforecast low cloud and although the exercise was a failure it confirmed the need for new

In at the start and active to the end. The Vickers Wellington was the mainstay of Bomber Command until the four-engined heavy bomber arrived.

First of the 'heavies'. The Short Stirling had a complex and frail undercarriage. Operating ceiling was poor although its bomb load was a great improvement on earlier aircraft.

After initial troubles, some of them caused by over-balanced rudders, the Handley Page Halifax, with its 13,000 lb bomb load, made a valuable contribution to the Bomber Offensive. It was in a Halifax of No. 10 Squadron that Don Bennett was shot down over Norway while trying to sink the German battleship 'Tirpitz'.

Air Vice-Marshal Sydney Bufton

Group Captain Harry (Hal) Bufton

Air Marshal Harris soon after his appointment as C-in-C Bomber Command and before his promotion to Air Chief Marshal. On the right is Air Vice-Marshal Robert Saundby, Senior Air Staff Officer under Harris who was responsible for the day-to-day running of Bomber Command.

Group Captain T. G. 'Hamish' Mahaddie, DSO., DFC., AFC., MC.

Air Vice-Marshal The Hon. Sir Ralph A. Cochran, KBE., CB., AFT.

The Avro Lancaster, certainly the most successful heavy bomber to be operated by any air force during World War II. In modified form it could carry a 22,000 lb. 'Grandslam' bomb which was more than 25 feet long.

The 'Wooden Wonder'. de Havilland Mosquitos were introduced into Pathfinder Force by Don Bennett against 'expert' advice. It proved almost uncatchable and the little aircraft could carry a larger bomb load to Berlin than the four-engined Boeing Flying Fortress.

methods of all-weather target finding. Nevertheless, confined as they were to non-electronic, steam-technology navigation Bennett's hand-picked crews soon worked up to a high level of proficiency. He laid on lectures, training sessions and discussions aimed at improving tactics. Typical of his professional approach, Bennett enlisted the help of Air Commodore Livingstone, senior RAF eye specialist. He provided special drops which dilated the pupils and improved the night vision of bomb aimers. Special anti-glare searchlight glasses were produced and Doctor McGowan, who was with Pathfinder Force throughout its existence, did much to improve the fitness of its aircrews.

Area bombing was the policy accepted by Harris for Bomber Command. It had certain advantages because, from experience, it was found that the destruction of gas, electric and water supplies in an industrial city caused more damage to war production than wrecking factories which were often quickly replaced by a number of smaller ones. Such bombing made lighter demands on the aircrews than, for example, the precision bombing of a factory that had to be located at night, often in foul weather and in the face of enemy night fighters or heavy ground defences. Unfortunately, by the time Pathfinder Force had been established GEE was being jammed by the Germans but other and better 'black boxes' were on the way. Meanwhile Bennett set about developing his Pathfinder techniques.

Although the Germans seemed able to produce better naval and artillery shells than the British for some reason they never matched the more exotic pyrotechnics used by the RAF. Various flares for illuminating the area and coloured Target Indicators for marking the aiming point had been proposed and initiated by Sydney Bufton some six months prior to the formation of Pathfinder Force. Don Bennett carried on where he left off.

The first real Pathfinder success came on the night of 28 August 1942 when 'Bennett's Air Force' marked targets at Nuremburg, a town of particular significance to the Nazis, with 250 lb red Target Indicators, so enabling the main bomber force to home in and inflict severe damage. A number of equally successful raids followed in quick succession while all this was encouraging the fact remained that targets still had to be found and marked visually. Introduce a little fog, haze or low cloud and accurate target marking became impossible. It was under such conditions that the main bomber force would often attack the nearest fire — and that was usually the wrong target or perhaps a German decoy.

Not long after the formation of Pathfinder Force Don Bennett got wind of a totally new precision radio aid. Those who should have encouraged such innovations had turned it down out of hand; the Master Airman immediately recognised its potential as a blind bombing aid. This is a remarkable example of the powerful influence a man of multi-talents can exert in times of war, for not only was Bennett an exceptional pilot and navigator; he was also a technical man of outstanding talent. Team responsible for the precision aid was headed by the late A. H. Reeves assisted by Dr. F. E. Jones. Early in the war their remarkable capabilities were put to the test when a Heinkel 111 twin-engine bomber was shot down. In it was found a radio receiver of a type unknown at the time. It operated on some rather unusual frequencies. The existence of a German 'beam' was suspected and later confirmed when a Luftwaffe prisoner in a 'bugged' cell was overheard bragging to a colleague that the British would never find it. The beam, code named *Knickebein* by the Germans, operated on a frequency of 31.5 MHz. No RAF equipment worked on this frequency band so a receiver of a type used by radio 'hams' was purchased from Webb's Radio Store in the Soho district of London and fitted into an Avro Anson belonging to the Blind Flying Research Flight at Boscombe Down. Wing Commander Bobby Blucke did much of the work himself, then Hal Bufton (younger brother of Sydney Bufton) and Corporal Mackie made ready to search out the enemy's secret beam. They took off from Wyton and headed out across England in the most appalling weather listening for morse signals that gradually merged to become a steady note. Sure enough, the beam existed and it was directed over the Rolls-Royce aero engine works at Derby. It was Reeves and Jones who set up decoy beam which misled the Germans into dropping their bombs in the Irish Sea instead of on Liverpool. Some by mischance fell on neutral Dublin.

Following their success with *Knickebein*, Reeves and Jones had this wonderful idea which apparently nobody wanted. It so happens that Hal Bufton and Wing Commander Colin McMullin(O.C. 109 Squadron), both of whom took an active part in finding the German *Knickebein* beam were aware of the work being done by Reeves and Jones. It was drawn to the attention of Don Bennett who immediately gave it his support. Much of the prototype construction was done at Wyton and the first set went into a Mk 16 Wellington.

Essentially the new aid consisted of a transmitter which

radiated pulses. These were received by the aircraft, amplified and returned to the ground station where equipment measured to an accuracy of micro seconds the time lapse between sending a pulse and receiving the return from the aircraft. Radio signals radiate at the speed of light and it is relatively easy to measure distances in this way to an accuracy of less than 50 yards. In effect the equipment could be set up to transmit an arc running through the target with the transmitter at its centre. The arc was only 17 yards wide and if the aircraft strayed to the left dashes were heard by the navigator; to the right dots came through the headset. Provided the aircraft flew around the 17 yard wide arc a steady note was heard. This, the tracking part of the equipment, was known as CAT.

A second transmitter advised the navigator when he was approaching the target. It sent out a letter B in morse when the aircraft had 8 minutes to run, followed by C when there were 5 minutes to target and then D at 3 minutes. At 5 seconds to bomb release there were five pips ending with a $2\frac{1}{2}$ second steady note when the Target Indicators or bombs (as the case required) were released. Codename of the distance-to-target transmitter was MOUSE and because the aid operated in the centimetre wavebound without producing a fixed beam the Germans were a long time in finding a countermeasure. By then an improved version was being fitted to Pathfinder aircraft and this was virtually unjammable.

They called the aid OBOE and even by present day standards it was a remarkable technical achievement, particularly having regard to the fact that it was devised in the early 1940s. A number of people, including some scientists who should have known better, ridiculed OBOE and did their utmost to have the project stopped. Don Bennett thought otherwise and, in the event, they were wrong and, as usual, he was right. Because OBOE was to prove one of the most important tools of Bomber Command. Without it the early failures of Bomber Command may have been prolonged except under ideal weather conditions, particularly during 1943 and the best part of 1944 when no other aid could approach its level of accuracy.

During December 1942 a trial raid was mounted against a target at Lutterade on the Belgian coast, using the original OBOE transmitters located at Trimingham, East Anglia and Walmer, Kent. Bombs were dropped to an accuracy of yards but an interesting fact emerged — the maps for that area were wrong and needed adjusting. The task was entrusted to Colonel Willis of

Ordance Survey who, incidentally, invented that much-loved character Pilot Officer Prune (someone else did the drawings). On 31 December S/Ldr H. Bufton marked a target at Dortmund for a small force of Lancasters, using Target Indicators on parachutes for the first time (the technique became known as sky-marking) and this was followed by more successful, OBOE-led raids. These encouraged Bomber Command to try OBOE target marking against Essen, where successful results, even with the aid of GEE, had eluded the RAF because of persistent smoke haze. Five crews laid down accurate markers and 442 heavy bombers spent the next forty minutes creating more damage than had been inflicted by all previous bombing raids. OBOE was Bennett's prodigy and it was confined to Pathfinder aircraft with 60 Group maintaining the equipment under Bennett's operational command. Wing Commander Finn was in charge of the OBOE ground controllers whose task it was to compute heading corrections based on the pulse returns being received from the aircraft. Under ideal conditions they could place an aircraft within a few hundred yards of the target. Harris was quick to grasp that here was an aid which could enable his command to bomb with accuracy even when the ground was obscured, but there were many problems for Bennett and his Pathfinders to solve before regular success could be achieved.

When Pathfinder Force was formed Bennett had a mixed bag of aircraft. There were Stirlings from 3 Group, Halifax bombers from 4 Group, the relatively new Lancaster (donated under pressure by 5 Group) and a collection of twin-engined Wellingtons, some of them with pressurised crew quarters. Stirlings were well enough liked by bomber crews but the main weakness was their poor operating altitude. A heavily loaded example was reluctant to climb and this made it relatively easy meat for the very accurate German anti-aircraft gunners. Bennett dealt with the matter by removing much of the armour plating. Also they did an analysis of how much ammunition was fired by the air gunners on a typical raid and saved a considerable amount of weight by reducing the number of rounds carried for each turret. But the Pathfinder fleet was anything but ideal. There was not enough standardisation. The maintenance problems facing Bennett's relatively small force as a result of having to carry spares for a catalogue of aircraft types was brought to the attention of Harris and within a few months Pathfinder Force was converted to Lancasters, the most outstanding heavy bomber to be produced on either side of the conflict.

Don Bennett had been acquainted with the OBOE experiments by Wing Commander Colin McMullen, a fellow Australian who commanded 109 Squadron. He also advised him to have a look at the Mosquito light bomber. As a night fighter the Mosquito had proved itself with distinction but Arthur Harris disliked the aircraft for a variety of reasons and refused to consider it for Bomber Command. He is alleged to have once written a memo during 1941 which said in effect "Anyone who supports having this wooden trash should be strung up from the highest lamp-post in Whitehall". Asked if there was any truth in this Harris, by then in his 92nd year and possessed of an excellent memory replied:-

"Of course, as you know it was a completely unarmed machine. And I had been long used in the service to the producers of aircraft boasting that they are about to build the best aircraft in the world. And when you were saddled with some of these things you found they were far from living up to the reputation given them by their manufacturers. And when I was told it had no armament, in the face of our losses, and it relied on running away - !"

Arthur Harris's views on the Mosquito were well known among senior officers of Bomber Command but following the tip-off from an ever well-informed W/Com. McMullen Bennett lost no time in visiting the de Havilland works at Hatfield where he flew one for the first time. So impressed was he with the remarkable little bomber that he took it back to Wyton and immediately engaged the C-in-C Bomber Command in an enthusiastic account of the Mosquito and its potential. Naturally Harris took some convincing but to his eternal credit the Air Marshal finally said "Oh well if you want them — try them". Eyebrows were raised in many quarters because not only was the Mosquito bomber version totally unarmed, it committed the cardinal sin of being built in wood at a time when metal was regarded as the only sane material for aeroplanes.

Bennett immediately ordered 50 of the early Mk IV version which could carry a bomb load of 2000 lbs although it was not long before this was doubled. He had plans for the Mosquito. Initially it would replace the Wellington 16s in 109 Squadron. He had disliked those aircraft, with their pressure cabins like ship's boilers, ever since an ill-fitting door came open and ruptured his ear drums. Whether or not he was authorised to order as many as 50 is not clear. But one day Bennett telephoned the Air Ministry and enquired "Have you any spare squadron numbers available?" much as one might ask for personalised car number plates. "What are you up to now?" demanded the suspicious voice at the other end. "Well I've managed to obtain some 'spare' Mosquitos and I want to form a few squadrons" Bennett explained. First 109 and then 105 Squadrons were re-equippped with them, then each squadron was given an additional flight enabling it to put up twelve Mossies (as they became universally known) over six targets on any one night. The Mosquito's potential as a fast, target marking aircraft was not lost on Bennett. At the time it was fast enough to be virtually uncatchable, particularly if it approached the target indirectly and created surprise. A fast aircraft carrying OBOE opened up all manner of new possibilities but most of the 'experts' shook their heads and told him that OBOE would never go into so small an aircraft. However, 109 Squadron personnel worked at the problem and proved them wrong. During the war practice bombs were not allowed to be dropped within Britain unless the ground could be seen but time was pressing and there was an urgent need to calibrate the new OBOE Mossies. Bombs were released from a great height and above clouds to prove the accuracy of the system but Pathfinder Force was breaking the law and everyone had to keep quiet about the tests.

The Mosquito proved to be an important addition to Pathfinder's arsenal. Not only could it mark targets in almost any weather but Bennett developed tactics that enabled the Mosquito to mislead the German night fighters. Then at a later stage he used them to set up his famous Light Night Striking Force about which more will be said in due course.

The Mosquito's detractors did not give up easily. While Bennett was introducing the little bomber at Pathfinder Force a high-powered meeting of 'experts' was called where it was almost unanimously agreed that the Mosquito could not be flown at night because of flashes from the exhaust system. These, it was claimed, were bright enough to inhibit the crew's night vision. Bennett informed the meeting that he found their comments interesting, even if he could not agree, because he had been flying the Mosquito at night for some time and he had managed without difficulty. He then let it be known that his engineering officer had visited the local blacksmith and got him to make some simple shields which fitted around the exhaust stacks. There was some embarrassed murmuring in the room, then the meeting broke up. Nothing more was heard about excluding the Mosquito from Bomber Command.

By the Autumn of 1942 Pathfinder Force had developed a number of techniques which were progressively and dramatically enhancing the accuracy of Bomber Command. Although early Pathfinder aircraft carried no better equipment than those of the main bomber force the introduction of OBOE and greatly improved Bennett-inspired training methods was opening up new possibilities. At first Pathfinder heavy bomber losses were running at a rate of more than 9 per cent, a loss rate in terms of crews and aircraft that could not be endured for long. But rapidly, as techniques improved, the loss rate dropped to 2.6 per cent and for the rest of the war it fluctuated between 1.5 per cent at its best and 4.5 per cent when times were bad.

Such was the impact of OBOE that when Krupps, the vital industrial complex situated in Essen, was repeatedly being bombed by the RAF through unbroken cloud cover, Hitler called a high-level meeting where he brushed aside suggestions from his experts who claimed that the British had a secret device. He even threatened to have them shot for holding such views. The RAF were bombing through gaps in the clouds, he insisted. Bennett regards OBOE as the single most effective instrument of warfare on the Allied side (the Americans later used OBOE in their aircraft).

Although much of his time was devoted to building up Pathfinder Force Bennett flew regularly. He had a Miles Whitney-Straight light aircraft for communications and aircraft fitted with new equipment were almost invariably tested by him. A typical example of his pilot skill was enacted on the occasion of his visit one evening to Boscombe Down. There he was to view from the air some new pyrotechnics. The Station Commander drove Bennett out to the flight line where a North American B25 Mitchell medium bomber stood ready along with its pilot, a Squadron Leader who seemed less than enthusiastic about what, in fact, proved to be one of the outstanding American bombers of the war. As they strapped in the Squadron Leader let it be known that he had never flown a Mitchell at night. Furthermore he regarded it as something of a hot rod, even when flown in daylight. It was a particularly dark night so Bennett had not even been able to take a look at the aircraft, which was completely unknown to him, but he told himself that if his neck was to be broken he would rather do the breaking himself. So he flew the aircraft, carried out the tests and landed. Several months later someone asked Bennett if he had ever seen a Mitchell and he replied "No, I have never actually seen a Mitchell — but I have flown one."

The role of pyrotechnics during the bombing offensive is often underestimated. Without good target indicators, which were difficult or even impossible to copy, Pathfinder Force could not have marked the target so that the main bomber stream coming up behind would recognise the aiming point with certainty. It had to be distinguished from the various fires and decoys set up by the enemy ground defences. The Germans would prepare a false target area, ring it with searchlights and guns to add realism, then let off incendiary devices to give the impression that a town was on fire although all this was taking place in open country. The aim was to induce RAF bomber crews to drop their loads without damaging the German war effort. When they did attempt to copy Pathfinder Target Indicators the result was lacking in conviction. As one ex-Pathfinder pilot recently commented "You could fall out of the aircraft laughing at them".

In furtherance of the need for better and still better pyros Bennett had discussions with the Ministry of Aircraft Production where Dr. W. Coxon was largely responsible for developing new, improved flares and Target Indicators. Much has been written in a number of excellent books about the various 'fireworks' that emerged and while a detailed description of these would be out of place in a biography it should be mentioned that some TIs released a shower of 60 twelve-inch candles; they fell to the ground to form a hundred-yard diameter circle which burned for three minutes. Alternatively the barometric fuse could be set to delay release of the candles until they had fallen nearer the ground to form a smaller but more intense circle, some 60 yards in diameter. Colours were green, red or yellow. Some TIs were arranged to burn in relays, changing colour twenty at a time while others of the large, single candle type, burned on impact changing colour after four of five minutes. The original 250 lb multi-coloured TIs were soon joined by a 4000 lb monster filled with a mixture of benzole, rubber and phosphorus which burned with a distinctive pink glow. These 'Pink Pansies' as they became known, were available to Pathfinder Force by September 1942. Then there was the Red Spot, a 250 lb case filled with cotton wool impregnated with a perchlorate/alcohol solution. This was burned on the ground as a dark red spot for about 20 minutes and provided a marker for precision bombing. Later a green version was produced. As an aid to avoiding German decoys some TIs featured an ingenious device which exhibited a two-letter morse signal. To discourage the German fire service and generally liven up the party explosive devices were later incorporated with the

Target Indicators and arranged to go off at intervals. At one stage they introduced a 1000 lb marker containing 200 candles but it suffered from poor ballistic characteristics and in consequence proved difficult to aim accurately. When later in the war German opposition was worn down by constant bombing daylight raids were resumed by the RAF and red, green, blue and yellow smoke puffs were introduced as Target Indicators. These burned for about 8 minutes and were very effective.

The Target Indicators so far described were released dropping freely to the surface when weather conditions allowed the ground to be seen. More often than not low cloud, fog or industrial haze meant that the target could only be located blind with the aid of OBOE. Then an ingenious system of sky marking was used and the TIs descended slowly on parachutes. The various target marking procedures developed by Bennett and his Pathfinder Force reached very high standards over a relatively short period. To a great extent he was assisted by Squadron Leader W. 'Basil' Rathbone, the Pathfinder Force Armament Officer who fortunately happened to be a director of Brocks, the famous firework manufacturers. Also Bennett, with the assistance of Sir Robert Renwick, had managed to establish a direct link with the Ministry of Aircraft Production so that he was able to obtain pyros and other equipment with a minimum of red tape.

By the end of 1942 improvements in bombing accuracy were so obvious that the value of Pathfinder Force was being acknowledged by all except those who, for their own personal reasons, felt moved to denigrate its great contribution to the war effort. Harris had originally regarded Pathfinder Force as an interim measure, a temporary collection of specialist crews which would find the targets until more bombers could be fitted with the up-and-coming 'black boxes'. By then his original scheme, allowing each group to do its own pathfinding, would take over. However the results being achieved by 'Bennett's Air Force' were compelling enough in themselves to make the C-in-C revise his plans. On 25 January, 1943 he ordered that Pathfinder Force be expanded. It was to become No. 8 Group and its present commander, Group Captain D. C. T. Bennett, DSO would be the Air Officer Commanding. At first he was made an Air Commodore but within a few months his rank would be brought into line with the other Group Commanders. Initially the Air Member for Personnel at Air Ministry refused to promote so young a man to Air rank, but Harris thumped the table and told him that Bennett was going to command the new Group on the same terms as others in his position. So they made him an Air Vice-Marshal. And he was yet to celebrate his 33rd birthday.

Chapter 9
Pathfinder Bennett

When Air Chief Marshal Sir Arthur Harris appointed Don Bennett as AOC 8 Group and made him an Air Vice-Marshal before his 33rd birthday he was taking no chances, far from it. The more disgruntled of wartime Britain's top brass may well have thought that Harris had taken leave of his senses but the C-in-C Bomber Command had good reason to pin his faith on the young Australian professional aviator. Some years previously he had recommended him for a job with Imperial Airways and, as recounted in earlier pages, his trust in Bennett had been totally justified. At the age of only twenty-six his prodigy had become captain of the largest type of civil aircraft flying at the time, he had broken the world's long distance record and then set up the Atlantic Ferry. Harris had every reason to be proud of his prodigy. Now he felt certain that, if he must endure a Pathfinder Force, Bennett was his man. True, other and more senior officers had been proposed for the job of AOC 8 Group but Harris was in no mood to have commanders forced on him by the Air Ministry. Relations with that august body at the time can only be described as 'strained'.

After a brief period in the rank of Air Commodore Don Bennett was made up to the same level as the other Group Commanders. There was an ugent need for more airfields and No. 8 Pathfinder Group eventually occupied Graveley, Oakington, Wyton, Bourn, Gransden Lodge, Upwood, Downham Market, Little Staughton and Warboys. A new headquarters was set up at Castle Hill House, Huntingdon — 8 Group had become a big operation. Apart from the Lancaster squadrons Bennett had a navigation training unit, a Mosquito conversion unit and a met flight.

Bennett's Senior Air Staff Officer was Group Captain (later Air Commodore) C. D. C. Boyce who had, in fact, served with him at a time before the war when they were both Flying Officers. Boyce did not always agree with Bennett or support him, so much so that those close to Don Bennett would on occasion warn him not to take for granted the loyalty of his SASO. Bennett was aware of this but he would counter these warnings with the words "Maybe you are right but he does a good job". And Boyce remained with Pathfinder Force to the end of the war.

Senior Administrative Officers came and went under Bennett. Many of these worthies spent their working days under the mistaken impression that the flying and operational branches existed for the benefit of administration. Clearly the reverse was, and indeed remains the case. Such attitudes were guaranteed to upset Bennett and it was not until the arrival of Group Captain H. McC. White that administrative tranquility descended on H.Q. 8 Group. He was to prove first class in every way.

A happy and fruitful liaison was struck with the appointment of Wing Commander (later Group Captain) C. F. Sarsby, a brilliant engineer who introduced Planned Maintenance to 8 Group long before it was adopted by other units, inside and outside Bomber Command. Bennett was fortunate in having him as Group Chief Engineering Officer; Sarsby was equally fortunate in working for a young AOC who knew enough of engineering to recognise the value of Planned Maintenance and who appreciated the outstanding talents he could bring to bear on the vital need of ensuring that Pathfinder crews could rely upon their aircraft. Sarsby helped Bennett standardise 8 Group, transforming it from a varied collection of aircraft to a highly efficient force based on the Lancaster and the Mosquito. A squadron consisted of 18 aircraft; Sarsby made it a point of honour always to have available for operations at least sixteen of them.

Group Intelligence was handled by Wing Commander W. J. R. Shepherd OBE. He had known Don Bennett during his days as a squadron commander at Leeming and, being impressed by his professionalism and sense of purpose, he had asked to join Pathfinder Force. As a highly specialised group, its main objective being the location of targets whatever the weather, navigation was something of a religion at 8 Group with Don Bennett in the role of High Priest. Of course there are many demands on a Group Commander's time so the day-to-day navigational well being of Pathfinder Force was in the hands of its Group Navigation Officer. It was an important post because an entire operation could depend on his ability to implant the highest levels of skill within his fellow navigators. The position of Group Navigation Officer was not a happy one at Pathfinder Force; several were lost on operations. Those who held this vital appointment were Squadron Leaders Buchan, Anderson, Price and Mitchell.

Group Armament Officer was Squadron Leader W. Rathbone. Part of his task was to produce special pyrotechnics and he became known as the 'Reluctant Dragon'. An important aid to intelligence and an effective monitor of bombing accuracy was photography. Bennett's determination to improve standards of photography were inspired by his dissatisfaction with existing methods when he was given his first squadron on re-joining the RAF after leaving Atlantic Ferry. In Squadron Leader H. W. Lees he had a brilliant photography expert and friendship between the two men continues to the present day, forty years after the return of peace.

Each RAF group had its own meteorologist. Bennett had personally appointed Mr. M. J. Thomas BSc as Pathfinder's Group Met Officer, but because of the wide variety of forecasts from within Bomber Command Bennett suggested that the met experts should hold a daily conference with a view to producing an agreed weather picture on which decisions could be based. These verbal met 'punch-ups' were conducted over a scrambled telephone network.

An important member of the Pathfinder Air Staff was the No. 1 Personnel Officer at 8 Group H.Q., Wing Commander T. G. Mahaddie. 'Hamish' Mahaddie, as he remains known to this day, was an ex-Halton boy apprentice who managed to re-muster from a technical trade and gain a pilot's course. He started the war as a Sergeant and flew on one of the first of the leaflet raids which took place over Prague. The Czechs were later to award him an M.C. but Hamish Mahaddie was commissioned on 1 April 1940 and in fact rose from Sergeant to Group Captain in a period of only two years. There was a hectic ten day period, at a time when he was still a Wing Commander, when he received a DSO, a DFC, an AFC and the Czech MC, some of them for events that had taken place many months previously. It was the custom for recipients of 'gongs' to buy drinks in the mess for their colleagues. During this period 'Hamish' Mahaddie seriously considered asking his bank for an overdraft.

In July 1942 he was posted to 7 Squadron, one of the founder units which made up the original Pathfinder Force before it attained Group status. Prior to that he had completed a tour of operations, flying Whitleys in 3 Group. Looking back of those days he recalled that:-

'My first tour was a complete and bloody waste of time — I was only pleased to survive it'.

Things were going to be very different for 'Hamish' Mahaddie now that he was in a professionally-orientated force. In 'Bennett's Air Force' the emphasis was on training, higher standards, more and still more training and the development of better methods. Early one morning W/Com. T. G. Mahaddie, DSO, DFC, AFC, MC (Czech) was summoned to the presence of Air Vice-Marshal Bennett DSO. He had just returned from a raid, tired, scruffy and ready for his bed.

'I landed at 5 am, — barely had time to have some breakfast and get tarted up. I had had no sleep but I went straight to see him. He was always very affable and very kind to me in his way and he said "I want you to be my Group Training Inspector". And he said "Go and find yourself an office" which I thought was a very good start'.

The interview occurred not long after the week in February 1943 when Mahaddie received his four medals. Possibly Bennett had this in mind when the interview recalled by Mahaddie continued in these terms —

'He also said to me — and this is something he has always denied — "You have come to me with a very good record. But I want you to know that your very, very best will hardly be good enough for me". I don't remember opening the door — maybe I crawled underneath. And I didn't know which way to turn when I got out. "Go and find yourself an office" he had said. And I helped build up Pathfinder from that minute. He [Bennett] gave me *carte blanche.*'

'Hamish' Mahaddie can best be described as a cherubic Scot with a fine sense of humour which is delivered, pious of manner, in a refined Edinburgh accent. After the war he became internationally known for his work in obtaining military aircraft for some of the leading film makers. During his Pathfinder days he would go around the various squadrons within Bomber Command, enticing the best talent to join 8 Group and warding off the natural hostility of squadron commanders who were about to lose their best crews with the magic words 'Pathfinder priority'. Everyone, including Mahaddie, genuinely believed that such priority existed. Only after the war was it made clear to all concerned — Pathfinder Force never did enjoy any special priority. In all, Mahaddie brought no fewer than 17,000 hand-picked aircrew officers and NCOs into Pathfinder Force. Not for nothing was he known as "Bennett's horse-thief'. Within a few months the original Pathfinder Force had grown into a large organisation. Bennett could be hard on his station commanders and they tended to change like the wind. It would be true to say that although not many of his personnel liked him he was admired practically without exception. On the other hand those who worked closely with him on a day-to-day basis, and were consequently better able to know their AOC, often developed a deep affection for the man. He would deal harshly with those who let down the force. On occasions below standard crews were sent back to their original groups and ordered to be off their Pathfinder station by 10 a.m. the following morning. But any member of Pathfinder who did his job knew if ever he was in trouble 'Able Oboe Charlie' (the phonetic alphabet used at the time for the letters AOC) would defend them, if necessary against the wrath of The Almighty.

Although target-finding techniques were constantly being refined and improved a typical Pathfinder operation would start with the usual briefing prior to the raid. Bennett always attended these briefings as well as the de-briefing at the end of the raid. It was found that the first aircraft to arrive over the target would be given hell by an enemy at peak alertness. Obviously the aim was to make it difficult for Pathfinder crews to mark the targets with any degree of accuracy. To help confuse the German defences at this stage of the raid, a force of relatively inexperienced crews, known as Supporters, would arrive in the area and drop high explosive bombs nearby. Because on many occasions the met service had proved to be unreliable Bennett pressed to have a weather flight under his direct command. Harris, C-in-C Bomber Command, agreed to this and henceforth Pathfinder Mosquitos conducted regular met flights, filling in gaps in the weather picture caused by the German occupation of Europe.

The risks faced by bomber crews, Pathfinder and Main Force alike, were many. They could be shot at over England, at the beginning or end of a raid, by an RAF night fighter pilot with poor aircraft recognition. On crossing the coast they could be fired on by the Royal Navy who, as a matter of principle, regarded all aircraft as hostile. Over the enemy coast there could be heavy flak, radar directed and very accurate. German night fighters were a constant hazard and there was the ever-present risk of flying in bad weather (RAF aircaft had no de-icing equipment and used to rely on a paste called Killfrost which was smeared over those areas of the aircraft most likely to be affected).

Over the target German flak could be positively frightening although, in practice, the odds were in favour of getting through without being hit. It was during the final run up to the target, when the aircraft had to fly on a steady track, that it was most at risk. Even after a Pathfinder crew had dropped its Target Indicators (or a Main Force aircraft had dropped its bombs) it was necessary to continue flying on a steady compass heading for another 20-30 seconds so that the camera could record the bomb burst below.

Probably more aircraft were lost to German night fighters during the return home than at any other phase of the raid. By then the crew would be tired and less alert. Finally, assuming the crew survived this catalogue of hazards there was always a risk of being shot down over the home base by a German intruder. Then there were the damaged aircaft with, perhaps, flaps that would not work, wheels (or a wheel) that could not be lowered or an engine on fire. Don Bennett regarded a raid against a heavily defended German target as the equivalent of taking part in the Battle of Jutland at sea, or a major land battle such as the action at El Alamein — and a bomber crew that survived one operational tour had to endure thirty such actions.

At one time there were fears that too many aircraft over the target area would present an unacceptable collision risk. There was also the added danger of higher-flying aircraft dropping bombs on their colleagues below. However, these fears were dispelled in the light of experience gained during the first really big raid mounted by the RAF shortly after Arthur Harris took over Bomber Command. On 30 May 1942 some 1000 aircraft bombed Cologne. They were carefully sequenced and a 'one-way-traffic' system previously arranged showed that a target could be saturated without serious risk of collision.

By the time Pathfinder Force had grown into a Group Bennett and his team had developed the target-finding technique to a fine art. There was a tendency for the actual bombing to scatter around the aiming point. The most persistent problem was a tendency for the main weight of the raid to drift back along the line of approach to the target. This was because bomb aimers had a natural tendency to bomb the first fire or coloured pyro that came within their bomb sight. Bennett introduced 'Backers-up' (later known as 'Visual Centres) and it was their task to re-mark the aiming point with a Target Indicator of another colour.

'Blockbuster', the massive 4000 lb 'cookie' that could be carried to Berlin by the little Mosquito.

A Mosquito of the Light Night Striking Force arriving home at sunrise.

Air Chief Marshal Arthur T. Harris

Target for Tonight – Don Bennett in conference.

Don Bennett (before his promotion to Air Vice-Marshal) with Queen Elizabeth (now the Queen Mother) during her visit to RAF Wyton in 1942. Hal Bufton, mainstay of the OBOE project, is on the right.

Behind the scenes heroes. If necessary the fitters and mechanics would work around the clock to keep 'their' aircraft serviceable. Picture shows Rolls-Royce Merlin engines of a Lancaster receiving attention.

"They have sown the wind – and they shall reap the whirlwind" said Arthur Harris of Germany soon after his appointment as C-in-C Bomber Command. In this picture a 'Blockbuster' is seen leaving the bomb bay of a Lancaster.

12,000 lb 'Tallboy' bomb of the kind that sank the German battleship 'Tirpitz' and took out Hitler's V3 gun, seen in this picture just after its release from the bomb bay.

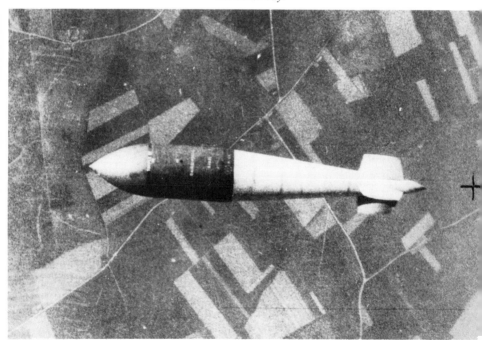

In April 1943 Pathfinder Force introduced the 'Newhaven' marking technique. It was an immediate success and Newhaven marking remained in use to the end of the war. Fifteen or so H2S-equipped aircraft would spearhead the raid by dropping flares simultaneously to light up a large area below. After two minutes Visual Markers flew over, identified the aiming point in the light of the flares and then marked it accurately with coloured Target Indicators. 'Backers-up' kept the TIs burning by dropping new ones at two minute intervals. Colour code adopted during 1943 was Yellow when the target had been marked with the aid of H2S (i.e. Blind Marking) Red when the target had been located visually and Green for the 'Backers-up' who were keeping the aiming point burning.

When weather conditions prevented Pathfinder crews from visually recognising the target another technique known as Parramatta (named after the birthplace of an Australian who was on Pathfinder staff) was used. H2S would locate the area and, in some cases, the actual target. Greater accuracy could be achieved when the raid was within OBOE range. Then the marking technique was called Musical Parramatta. And if the target area was obscured by cloud, fog or industrial haze they had a 'skymarking' technique which entailed dropping TIs on parachutes in a position above ground through which the bomb should pass on its way to the target. Surprisingly accurate resluts were obtained from this method which was given code name Wanganui after the home town of a New Zealand officer who worked with Don Bennett.

Bennett was responsible for planning Pathfinder tactics and these would naturally vary according to the weather and known defences. On occasions, important turning points on the route would be marked with a coloured flare. Yet another flare might be dropped at a point say, 15 miles from target. Main force bomber crews would time their run to the target from that point as an added safeguard against bombing a German decoy.

Bennett always regarded the route to and away from the target as vitally important if losses were to be contained. He devised an elaborate and brilliant system of setting up 'spoof' raids. A special Mosquito unit, known as the Light Night Striking Force, was established to mount false raids intended to draw away the German night fighters while the main bomber force flew towards a town only to swing away at the last moment and head for the intended target. Don Bennett is naturally proud of the role played by his LNSF and the success of his complex tactics.

Unfortunately, other voices within Bomber Command had the ear of its C-in-C and the advice of Bennett was, on occasion, over-ruled with disastrous results.

It should be remembered that Bennett was some twenty years younger than the other group commanders and apart from his old boss, A. V. M. 'Roddy' Carr, there was some resentment of the young Australian who was too professional by half for their liking. To some extent the friction may have been increased by Bennett pressing to have things done his way. Interviewed for this book in November 1983 Marshal of the RAF Sir Arthur Harris said of Bennett — "He liked to do everything his way. And his own way generally proved to be the best way". Was the brilliant Don Bennett difficult to control? "No. People say I used to have a lot of arguments with him which is quite true. My staff had arguments with him, and then I had one way or another to reconcile them".

Looking back on the situation as it existed during the Pathfinder era it seems likely that much of the friction was the result of the great Arthur Harris's loyalty and almost blind trust in two officers who had served under him as flight commanders in Mesopotamia in 1924. One was Robert Saundby who during the war became Harris's right hand man at Bomber Command HQ; he was virtually responsible for the day-to-day running of the Command. The other was The Hon. Ralph A. Cochran, an austere officer who rarely displayed any trace of humour. In Bennett's period with Pathfinder Force Cochran was AOC 5 Group. The two men did not get on. Those who remember the period feel that Cochran regarded Don Bennett as a young upstart while Bennett felt the older man would have been a far more useful AOC had he taken part in half a dozen raids so that he could understand the problems facing his bomber crews. Of all Air Chief Marshal Sir Arthur Harris's Group Commanders only Bennett had operational experience. Air crew who served under Cochran when he was AOC of 5 Group thought well of him although there were times when he would adopt an abrupt and perhaps bullying approach as a cover for his lack of knowledge or experience of modern bombing techniques. There can be little doubt, having regard to the opinions of many who were a part of the action during the period 1942-45, that Arthur Harris did pay too much attention and accept almost without question the views of Cochran. Some are convinced that there were occasions when the position adopted by Cochran was motivated by a desire to oppose Bennett rather than establish the right course of action. If this is true, and it is now almost impossible to prove one way or the other, then the nation in general, and Bomber Command in particular were to pay dearly for the vanity of man. Bennett is convinced that Cochran had excessive influence over the C-in-C Bomber Command and to a considerable extent Sir Arthur Harris himself seemed to confirm the substance of Bennett's complaint when in November 1983 he was asked if he had automatically supported Cochran against Bennett.

"I think he [Bennett] is being a little bit fictitiously sensitive. But it is quite true that nine times out of ten I would support Cochran over anybody. Because when I had 45 Squadron in Mesopotamia I was lucky enough to have what I have always claimed were the two most experienced and best flight commanders in the service — Cochran and Saundby. I had complete confidence in Cochran, but mind you any difference of opinion I might have had with Don Bennett in the Cochran/Bennett time was, I think, that I knew Cochran very well and I had long experience of his abilities. Bennett was a brand new boy come up from 'the wild and woollies', from Australia — and he wore an odd uniform and wasn't in the same service!"

The last words were not spoken very seriously but in general the answer given by Arthur Harris, surely one of the finest senior commanders of any service in World War 2, shows him to have been subject to the same human frailties as most of us. He would describe Cochran as "A most brilliant, enthusiastic and hard-working leader of men", yet the Air Vice-Marshal had no contemporary flying experience and his first hand knowledge of bombing operations did not exist. When Sydney Bufton was at the Air Ministry he had an unexpected visit by Cochran on the day he was appointed AOC 5 Group. He came down from Portal's (Chief of Air Staff) office and without so much as a 'Good Morning' demanded "What are the targets?" When asked "Which targets" he blustered "Come on — come on, the targets". Even after Bufton had run through the various categories of target (industrial, oil, naval etc) Cochran was still unable to say what he was looking for.

Bufton felt that all group commanders should have flown but Arthur Harris had issued a firm order to the effect that none of his Air Vice-Marshals should fly on operations. Rumour had it that Bennett consistently ignored this instruction. He would be over the target area, sitting high above the main bomber activity in his Mosquito, then first home to be present at the de-briefing and in possession of the conduct of the raid in some detail. This used to mystify the crews. Officially Bennett completed about twenty operational sorties but was it true that he disregarded the C-in-C Bomber Command and used to sit above raids taking notes?

'It's true and I don't really want to talk about it. I did it occasionally — I was caught out once by a Mosquito Squadron Commander, not a Pathfinder, who actually saw me. He said "You were there" and I replied "Keep your big mouth shut" and that was that'.

Was he not in serious breach of service discipline in disregarding the orders of his Commander in Chief? Bennett's view is that even at Group Commander level little if any highly secret information was known. By at least witnessing a few raids at first hand they would have more fully understood some of the problems confronting the bomber crews. And had a few Group Commanders been killed or taken prisoner Bomber Command would have benefited from an influx of new blood and fresh ideas. As it was, 5 Group had Cochran and in Bennett's view —

"Cochran was a disaster. He would have been the best Group Commander in Bomber Command had he done ten trips — or if he had done any trips. But his knowledge of flying and of operations was nil".

While there may well have been a lot of truth in this assessment the fact remains that 5 Group was well run and very successful. So Cochran must have had his talents.

One day Arthur Harris rang Bennett at his Pathfinder HQ and said "Look, I've got an idea and I would like your opinion of it. I am proposing to send twelve Lancs from Five Group and twelve Lancs from Three Group on a sneak-through raid to Berlin. With only twenty-four aircraft they can surprise the defences and get through". It was a clear moonlit night so Bennett replied "It sounds crazy to me". "Oh, you think so do you" retorted Harris. Don Bennett explained that the whole of the German fighter force would be able to concentrate on a handful of RAF bombers. He predicted a 70 per cent casualty rate. "Well I'm going to do it" Harris replied. It later transpired that the AOC of 5 Group, at the time Air Vice-Marshal W. A. Coryton CB. MVO (later Air Chief Marshal Sir Alec Coryton) had refused to send his Lancasters on the raid where-upon Harris immediately sacked him. Cochran, on the other hand, agreed with the project and he was made AOC 5 Group in place of Coryton whom

Bennett regarded as one of the best senior officers in Bomber Command.

Taken overall Bomber Command losses fluctuated widely during various stages of the war. For example when 617 Squadron made its legendary raid against the German dams, flooding much of the industrial Ruhr, 42 per cent of the aircraft were lost. Yet on more normal bombing operations against the Ruhr losses over a considerable period average only 4.7 per cent. Much depended on tactics, surprise and saturating the German defences. For example, almost 3100 sorties were flown against Hamburg between 24 July and 4 August 1943. For the first time, great quantities of aluminium foil strips were dropped, a technique given the code name Window which swamped the German radar network, threw their night fighter force into utter confusion and resulted in the almost total destruction of Germany's second city. RAF losses were only 2.8 per cent but such was the devastation that Albert Speer, the brilliant Reichminister for Industry, warned Hitler that if the British were to mount similar raids on five or six more major cities, Germany would be out of the war. The news fell on deaf ears; Hitler would not even meet rescue workers from Hamburg, let alone visit the stricken city.

When the Luftwaffe was at the height of its power it managed to destroy 5 per cent of Coventry. At the time this was regarded as a scale of destruction on the threshold of human endurance. Harris learned much from these German raids and when Pathfinder Force had perfected its target-marking techniques RAF Bomber Command was able to seriously damage eighty per cent of some German cities. Many are of a similar opinion to that expressed by Albert Speer to Hitler; Bomber Command on its own could have knocked Germany out of the war. Yet even by 1944 Harris had been given no more than one third of the bombers originally planned for his command and only 45 per cent of his still limited force could be employed against Germany because he was constantly being pressed to undertake other tasks. Harris always maintained that if Bomber Command had been given its 1944 aircraft strength a year earlier, and if it had been allowed to concentrate without interruption on German towns along with the American bomber force, there would have been no need for the Normandy landings and the subsequent hard slog across France, Belgium and Germany itself. The Fatherland would have succumbed to the effects of constant air raids as indeed did Japan not long after the end of the war in

Europe. Some would argue that it was the atom bomb that put Japan out of the war but this factor was only the last straw that broke the Imperial Forces' will to fight. The two atom bombs represented only 3 per cent of America's total bombing effort against Japan. In the light of this, and the views expressed by Albert Speer, it is tempting to ask why Bomber Command was not directed to finish the war, leaving the Allied ground forces to carry out no more than a police operation afterwards. Harris was in no doubt about the reason.

'I think it was the Joint Chiefs of Staff who didn't feel they would like to be responsible for reversing an old order of things. After all the whole of the Army had been brought up with the idea of land warfare. And to suddenly tell them that they are not wanted any more, because land warfare is out, is naturally enough bound create a tremendous howl of anguish and every conceivable sort of opposition'.

Was it not true that towards the end of the war the RAF and the American Air Force knocked the fighting spirit out of the German Army?

'It was absolutely true. And when I say that I am supported by the only two people who really matter — Rommel and, believe it or not, Monty'.

The strength of Bomber Command would in itself have been of little effect but for its eyes and ears — Pathfinder Force. A typical illustration of the vital role performed by 'Bennett's Air Force' was the Ruhr, industrial heart of Germany, essential to its war needs and supplier of materials to most of its diversified armament industry. Harris was forever plagued with suggestions from self-appointed 'experts' who pressed for the bombing of this or that 'panacea' target which, at one stroke, would put Germany out of the war. It is very doubtful if such targets existed but loss of important factories in the Ruhr would certainly have been very serious for the Axis powers.

It so happened that the geographical location of the Ruhr towns afforded them more or less constant protection by their own smoke and industrial haze which hung in the valley and made accurate location from the air extremely difficult. Early raids, even of 1000 bomber scale, had done little damage. Then on the night of 5 March 1943 Pathfinder Force took a hand. Five Mosquitos dropped red Target Indicators on the aiming point. Also 15 miles from the target yellow flares were positioned to guide in the main force of 407 bombers and the raid that followed was over in 40 minutes. A remarkable incident during this raid was experienced by Flying Officer F. J. Garvey and his crew when a 4000 lb bomb dropped from their aircraft was hit by German flak. It exploded, showering the bomber with debris and starting a small fire which was quickly brought under control. Subsequent photo reconnaissance revealed that for the first time serious damage had been inflicted on the Ruhr. It was the shape of things to come. By July 1943 Bennett had two OBOE facilities working and these enabled him to maintain a stream of 'backers-up' re-marking targets throughout the raids. On 25 July an attack employing his improved OBOE precision location was mounted against the Krupps industrial complex. Out of 190 workshops 110 were seriously damaged or totally destroyed. When next morning Dr. Gustav Krupp visited the ruins of his great industrial empire he collapsed in a fit from which he never fully recovered.

Yet another example of the essential role played by Pathfinder Force was its spearheading of the highly successful raid, carried out with great precision, against the secret research centre at Peenemünde where Hitler's V1 and V2 weapons were being developed. The raid took place on 17 August, 1943 and a new Target Indicator (Red Spot) capable of exceptionally accurate aim, was used for the first time. So damaging was the raid to Germany's secret missile programme that General H. Jeschonnek, Luftwaffe Chief of General Staff, committed suicide.

Bomber Command successes and the essential role it played in final victory have already filled the pages of many excellent books. But even those who did not particularly care for Don Bennett are quick to acknowledge that without his brilliance and technical skill even the dynamic 'Bomber' Harris would have been unable to attain the level of success that was eventually achieved by Bomber Command. Typical of the comments one is likely to hear from critics of Don Bennett are those of Air Chief Marshal Sir Wallace Kyle DFC, one time Governor of Western Australia who, as a wartime Group Captain, commanded a Pathfinder station.

'He [Bennett] was very rude to me and being a fellow Australian I was even ruder back. But I would be the first to admit that without Bennett, 'Bert' Harris could never have done his job.'

Wallace Kyle was not alone in his appraisal of Don Bennett as a wartime leader of exceptional talent. His views were largely shared by the German High Command. In document "No. 61008

Secret Ic/Foreign Air Forces West" issued early in 1944 by Luftwaffenfuhrungsstab Ic/Fremde Luftwaffen West to all units of the German Luftwaffe down to Group level they freely acknowledge "The success of a large-scale night raid by the RAF is in increasing measure dependent on the conscientious flying of the Pathfinder crews". The document describes Don Bennett as "a 35-year-old Australian — known as one of the most resourceful officers of the RAF". It goes on to list his pre-war achievements and the part he played in setting up Atlantic Ferry Command. The document (which spells his name with one 't' throughout) claimed that "Bennet's appointment as 'Commander of the Pathfinder Formations' is also based on the fact that he has written two standard books on astro-navigation". According to this document, the Germans had assumed that as bomber crews came to rely more and more on the Pathfinder Force so their navigational skill would decline but it acknowledges they were wrong in believing this.

In a long and varied career, most if it conducted with considerable skill and intellect, many are of the opinion that Pathfinder Force was Don Bennett's finest achievement . What was it like to serve in Bennett's Air Force? Some varied impressions are recounted in the next chapter.

Chapter 10
The Fear and the Laughs and the Tears

It is a long established fact that the success or failure of any organisation, big or small, is almost invariably influenced from the top. True, that elusive ingredient, luck, plays a role in the outcome of any enterprise but some leaders of men have a talent for making their own luck. In looking back on the remarkable success of Pathfinder Force, and its major contribution to the effectiveness of Bomber Command under the masterly leadership of Air Chief Marshal Sir Arthur Harris, the genius and drive of Don Bennett shines forth, burning brightly like one of his own Target Indicators. What was it like to be a part of No. 8 (PFF) Group? At its height it was a big organisation with 8 Lancaster squadrons, 11 Mosquito squadrons (many of them in Bennett's spoof-raid organisation, the Light Night Striking Force) as well as a met flight, a navigation training school and conversion units for Lancasters and Mosquitos.

War is a serious business, particularly when a relatively small nation such as Britain finds itself fighting another country that has planned for the domination of Europe, or perhaps even more areas of the world, and armed accordingly. Nevertheless, war is seldom unrelieved fear and sadness. There are lighter moments which stand out in contrast to appear hilarious at the time. The following accounts of day-to-day life in Pathfinder Force include comments and opinions from those within and outside 8 Group.

*   *   *   *

During the war airfields appeared, like mushrooms growing on a sheep field, in a frantic effort to accommodate the growing number of RAF and American squadrons. Occasionally runways were sited without due regard to local conditions, one such airfield being Little Staughton, Cambridgeshire, where those responsible had contrived to build the main runway directly in line with a very tall church steeple. Station commander at the time was Group Captain R. W. P. Collings DFC (who had commanded the first Halifax squadron some years previously). After a number of aircraft had narrowly missed impaling themselves on the church weathercock he rightly formed the view that the steeple was a hazard to shipping, to use a maritime expression.

Collings visited the local vicar and politely but firmly said "Look, I'm terribly sorry vicar but I'll have to take your church down". Not unnaturally the poor man of the cloth was horrified and he dashed to see the Bishop of Ely who in turn asked to see 'Hamish' Mahaddie, a senior Pathfinder officer who at the time commanded RAF Warboys in addition to his other duties as Bennett's Inspector of Training. The story is explained in the refined Edinburgh accent of that ex-pillar of the Pathfinder Force.

'He [the Bishop of Ely] came one day in his gaiters and kilt. And he was standing at the bar when one of the young bucks said "Perhaps you would like a drink sir". And his eyes lit like Target Indicators on a barrel of Guinness. We used to send a Mossie to Ireland every week for barrels of Guinness for which we made special slings so they could be carried in the bomb bay. He said "Yes — if that's Guinness I would like just a wineglass full". So they gave him a large schooner which they only half filled with Guinness but half filled with Port. He said "It is so long since I have had this. Would you mind if I had another"? Well he never asked a bloody question about the church and the next thing I heard it was razed to the ground. But I got all the stained glass windows and I made a pub out of them on my station. Collings was furious that I did this'.

*   *   *   *

Don Bennett's early appreciation of the Mosquito has already been mentioned. Originally it was anticipated that losses with these aircraft on Pathfinder duties might run high, perhaps 9 per cent. In the event the figure settled at around only one-and-a-half per cent so Bennett found himself with surplus Mosquitos. With them he fitted out 139 Squadron and this became the spearhead of his remarkable Light Night Striking Force. Much of its work entailed setting up decoy raids to mislead the German defences and draw away the night fighters from the main bomber force, but during one phase of the war it made bombing raids to Berlin on 43 consecutive occasions without a break. Sometimes the same aircraft would make a second raid on the same night. The LNSF used to operate in the most appalling weather and one night Don Bennett was visited by Mrs. Ogden Reid of the *New York Herald Tribune.* She had asked to witness the start of a raid. This distinguished lady of the American press arrived with a member of the British Government and was immediately driven to the end of the runway by Bennett. Fog caused heavy bomber raids to be cancelled but as the mist swirled around the signal caravan at the end of the runway Mosquitos could be seen taxying on from both directions to save time, lining up and taking off for Berlin in quick succession. She turned to Bennett and said "I see they have got a bulge — they're carrying a 'Blockbuster' are'nt they?" She asked what it weighed and Bennett told her 4000 lbs which was 500 lbs more than a B-17 Flying Fortress could carry to Berlin. In any case, he pointed out, a Fortress would not accommodate a 4000 lb 'cookie' because it was too large for its bomb bay. The famous Press lady pondered for a few moments before replying "I only hope the American public never realises these facts."

The Light Night Striking Force flew 553 sorties during April 1943 for the loss of only one aircraft. One young Mosquito pilot of those days was Wing Commander I. G. Broom (later Air Marshal Sir Ivor Broom DSO, DFC and two bars, AFC).

'We did 25 nights to Berlin. You could fly there and be back in the mess before the bar closed. We could carry more to Berlin with a crew of two in a Mosquito than could a Flying Fortress with a crew of ten. They had to fight their way there and back in daylight. We went fast at night, at 28,000 ft.'

* * * *

Although radio aids to navigation have existed in various forms since the early days of flying the problems of landing in fog have only in recent years been solved with the introduction of autoland. During the war the approach aid was called Standard Beam Approach, a radio facility that bombarded the pilot with dots and dashes which he received through his headset unless the aircraft was 'on the beam' when a steady note was heard. Even in expert hands SBA required some visibility during the final stages of a landing. Later Ground Controlled Approach (GCA), a radar device operated by skilled ground-based operators, was able to talk down pilots in poor weather but when a great number of aircraft had to be landed in quick succession the aid was too slow.

A crude but effective answer to the problems of landing in fog came with the introduction of FIDO (Fog, Intensive Dispersal Of). In essence it consisted of a length of burners running down each side of the runway. When the aircraft returned home in fog, petrol by the ton was pumped into the burners which generated heat sufficient to disperse fog above and to either side of the runway, at the same time providing a vivid red glow which guided the pilot during his final approach.

One of the first installations was at RAF Graveley, a Pathfinder station near Huntingdon, and one night Air Vice-Marshal Bennett decided to sample FIDO in a Miles Whitney Straight light 'plane which he kept for short trips from station to station. Group Captain Mahaddie was instructed to share with his AOC the pleasure of flying for the first time between two mile-long troughs of flames. It was a wooden aircraft and 'Hamish' Mahaddie was less than enthusiastic about the occasion which he described some forty years later:-

'And this glow gets redder and redder and redder. We are getting lower and I am watching that bloody altimeter until we seem to be almost on the ground — sixty feet or something like that. Then we burst through and there are these flames, burning away as far as the eye can see. He [Bennett] lands, then he does a roller, takes off and comes around, flying under the cloud this time. We flew back to Wyton where there was no FIDO and a cloud base of only a few hundred feet. And it doesn't bother Bennett at all. But by Christ it bothered me'!

That evening Don Bennett repeated the performance in a Lancaster and all the fire brigades within thirty miles rushed to RAF Graveley. They thought the entire station was on fire.

* * * *

Early in 1942 a young lad by name of Maxwell Rankin (now Doctor A. M. Rankin) left school in the hope of joining the Royal Australian Air Force. He was too young so a job was taken in an 'unprotected' activity so that he could get into uniform at the first opportunity. Two years later he was accepted into the RAAF and trained as a navigator. During one leave he went back to see his old boss who casually told him that his son was in the RAF. He mentioned the fact with obvious pride but great modesty, at no time mentioning that his son was an Air Vice-Marshal. The firm

— G. T. Bennett & Co. of Queen Street, Brisbane. The ex-boss — Mr G. T. Bennett. And not once did he mention that his youngest son was AOC Pathfinder Force, spearhead of Bomber Command.

* * * *

On 28 July 1944 S/Ldr. J. F. Slade was on his 58th operational flight when he was hit by flak over Hamburg. The left wing broke from the outer engine nacelle and folded upwards whereupon a slow spiral descent developed. By reducing engine power on the right-hand engines and holding on right rudder the situation was brought more or less under control. Attempts to jettison the remaining Target Indicators and 1000 lb bombs created new problems as the bomb doors were opened, drag increased and the aircraft lost height. So they headed out over the North Sea and eventually crossed the English coast at only 1500 feet. Slade had tried a 'dummy' landing while approaching England and he was dismayed to find that his Lancaster had a stalling speed of 140 knots — about double the normal figure for an example flying at light weight.

He touched down on the emergency runway at Woodbridge, the left undercarriage leg folded, the stricken Lancaster skidded off the runway and promptly broke up. Unbelieveably the entire crew got out unhurt.

* * * *

Major Swales, an officer in the South African Air Force seconded to 8 Group, was hit by a German night fighter while acting as a Master Bomber on a raid. The Lancaster burst into flames but he remained at the controls so that his crew could bale out. By the time they had all departed he was too low to save himself and he died at the controls.

* * * *

Group Captain 'Hamish' Mahaddie used a massive board to keep track of his crews. Each Morning at 8 his sergeant would have the depressing task of removing the names of those who had not returned from the previous night's operations. Fortunately Pathfinder Group always had a great reservoir of talent on which to draw for new flight commanders and squadron commanders.

However in Mahaddie's view, and that of the Pathfinder Senior Air Staff Officer, Air Commodore Boyce, among Bennett's many talents was not one for selecting people. According to Mahaddie, an otherwise unreserved admirer of his old chief, "Bennett should have been forbidden by Act of Parliament from selecting anybody — he was no good at it at all." In consequence he and Boyce, a large, bear-like man who was known by his colleagues as 'Bruin', would first agree on possible candidates for the job of flight or squadron commander. Perhaps three names would be considered and their favourite would be presented last to Don Bennett in the certain knowledge that he would find fault with the first two. Whereupon Boyce would say "well you've turned down the best ones and that only leaves Squadron Leader 'X'. And if you choose him you had better find yourself a new SASO." Bennett would then automatically say "put him in Hamish."

It was after one of these pantomimes that Boyce and Mahaddie closed Bennett's door behind them. They were shaking hands with undisguised glee when suddenly their AOC came out. He saw them looking very pleased with themselves and naturally enough said "What"s this"? to which Hamish replied, with great presence of mind, "It's Bruin's birthday." "Ah, Bruin, come in tonight and have a drink" replied Bennett. Bruin Boyce was not on good terms with his young AOC at the time and he was so furious with the situation in which Mahaddie had landed him that they were not on speaking terms for weeks afterwards.

*   *   *   *

5 Group is often credited with having invented the Master Bomber concept. In fact the idea came from several people in Pathfinder Force who felt there was a need for a very experienced bomber pilot to direct the raid from above using his radio to correct errors, the most common being 'creepback' from the aiming point. They proposed the name 'Raid Commentator', but Air Chief Marshal Sir Arthur Harris was against the idea so it was not approved. Not long afterwards Pathfinder Force learned that 5 Group was using their idea and calling it 'Master Bomber'.

Flight Lieutenant Alex Thorn, DSO, DFC, was a Master Bomber. He would cruise around over the raid, advising the 'Backers-up' where they should drop their Target Indicators and instructing the main force to ignore this fire and bomb that.

'We were always afraid of the collision risk but statistics showed that it was very slight. I could never believe it at the time but I have no personal experience, and I don't know anybody who has, of seeing a collision. Spirit was wonderful in Pathfinders. Losses were lower than average, partly because they were all hand-picked crews. There were a great many ex-flying instructors among the pilots. There was always a friendly rivalry between 8 and 5 Group. The undercurrent was felt down to a low level.'

Alex Thorn was in 635 Squadron at Downham Market where the Station Commander was 'Digger' Kyle. Early in 1945 a daylight raid was mounted on Osnabruck. Thorn and his other crew members clambered aboard the Lancaster and he started the engines. The gauges indicated that very little fuel was in the tanks. Now this was very strange because the all-important maintenance and serviceability document that had to be signed by air and ground crew before each flight (Form 700) showed that the tanks had been filled.

Being the Master Bomber on this raid, Alex Thorn decided to ignore the fuel gauges and go. In those days contents gauges could be temperamental so perhaps they were lying. In any case the main force would soon be on its way.

They taxied a few yards and then one of his crew said "This is bloody silly — I think you should get those tanks checked." So Alex stopped and had them dipped — they were almost empty. It later transpired there had been a serious misunderstanding between two of the ground crew. Now time was pressing and they were faced with a 20 minute delay while the tanks were filled. So the seven-member crew, encumbered with parachutes and other equipment, jumped out of the Lancaster and dashed across to the spare aircraft only to find that its radio was not working. The by now fuming crew ran back to the original bomber and waited for the petrol bowser to pump away and deliver fuel while precious minutes floated away. By the time Alex Thorn and his crew were getting airborne the main bomber force was half way to the target, so to arrive in time he was forced to accept the risks of flying direct towards Osnabruck; there was no time for flying dogleg courses to confuse the German defences.

A few weeks later he did a daylight raid on Nuremberg and their Lancaster was badly shot up. For this he was awarded his DSO. 'I know it was really for the Osnabruck raid but they couldn't put in the citation what the reason was'. How could they have said 'Because Flight Lieutenant Thorn was delayed when they forgot to put petrol in his Lancaster he was forced to risk flying direct to the target without the support of other aircraft'.

* * * *

Ground crew were proud of their aircraft to the point where they resented pilots who treated their pampered flying hardware with anything less than unreserved reverence. Corporal J. W. Roberts remembered the occasion when Air Vice-Marshal Bennett visited RAF Upwood during 1944 and strapped himself into 'his' Mosquito.

'I always observed the aircrew I met with an eye to how good they were or otherwise — and AVM Bennett *was* good. He exuded confidence, went through the drills quickly but correctly, warmed up the engines with sympathy, tested the flaps up, down and set, bomb doors shut, controls checked and then chocks away — all in one smooth, overlapping routine. He taxied off at a good pace and was belting down the runway in one flowing sequence. As he got to the speed of no return his port engine gave a hell of a bang, and I thought that's a write-off. Not so; the aircraft veered slightly, the rudder was hard round, the prop feathered, and he took off. He did one circuit and landed perfectly. Instead of dumping the aircraft he taxied round to me on one engine then said all that was necessary, no more. Ten minutes later he was airborne in another aircraft and you would never have guessed he had just experienced a nasty moment.'

Corporal Roberts remembered a Mosquito taking-off in the early evening for a trip to Berlin. Less than four-and-a-half hours later it was back being re-fuelled and bombed up for a second trip. Such double trips to Berlin within a single night were not uncommon in the Light Night Striking Force set up by Don Bennett.

* * * *

Bennett as seen by others:-
'He was a chap with very demanding operational standards and he would not ask anyone to do anything he was not capable of himself. He didn't perhaps realise that some people were not as good as he was.'

(Air Marshal Sir Ivor Broom, DSO, DFC** AFC)

Lancaster of No. 467 Australian Squadron based at Waddington with ground crew celebrating its 100th operational bombing sortie. This aircraft is now exhibited in pristine condition at the RAF Bomber Command Museum, Hendon near London.

Christmas party at RAF Gransden Lodge, 1943. On the left is Group Captain R. W. P. Collings DFC (Station Commander at Little Staughton). Next to him is Group Captain Johnnie Fauquier, DSO., DFC., the famous Canadian bomber pilot. On Ly Bennett's left is Group Captain Dunlop, Station Commander at Gransden Lodge and Don Bennett with some of his pilots.

End of War celebrations at RAF Wyton. On the scaffold are Messrs. Mussolini, Hitler and Tojo. The Bennett children are there and Don Bennett is acting as host to a party of Russian officers.

Lord Winster with Don Bennett opening London (Heathrow) Airport on 1 January, 1946. Ly Bennett may be seen in the picture wearing a fur coat.

*'Star Light' was the first Lancastrian to enter service with BSAA. On 1
December, 1945 it became the first commercial aircraft to use the new London
(Heathrow) Airport.*

*On 1 January, 1946, 'Star Light' (Lancastrian G-AGWA) embarked on a
route proving flight from Heathrow to Buenos Aires via Lisbon, Bathurst,
Natal, Rio de Janeiro and Montevideo. From left to right are Radio
Superintendent McGillavry, Donald Bennett, StarGirl Guthrie (first stewardess
to join the airline) and, recently out of the RAF, Wing Commanders Cracknell
and Alabaster, both of them Captains under training.*

Preparing 'Star Light' for its route proving flight. This first international departure from Heathrow was flown by Donald Bennett.

G-AGSU was the prototype Avro Tudor 2. On 23 August, 1947, it crashed while taking-off from the factory airfield at Woodford, killing Roy Chadwick, its brilliant designer, and test pilot Bill Thorn. The aileron controls had been incorrectly connected.

'In the Pathfinder Force you didn't go to Bennett and say "Can I do this?" Bennett was a guy who "did it" — so everybody "did it." I think he was wrong in his attitude towards gunners. He wasn't as good on gunnery as he was in every other facet. Bennett is nothing if not absolutely honest as a person. He is not capable of dishonesty in any way'.

(Group Captain 'Hamish' Mahaddie, DSO, DFC. AFC, MC (Czech)

'He had his secretary with him and when he got into his aircraft he started dictating his notes of what he had done during the day. I think he had a dictating machine. I thought the man meant business and knew what he was doing. He impressed me as someone completely dedicated to his work — forward-looking — modern thinking.'

(Group Captain Leonard Cheshire, VC, DSO** DFC)

*　　*　　*　　*

On 1 January 1945 Wing Commander Broom (later Air Marshal Sir Ivor Broom DSO, DFC** AFC) took his Mosquito squadron on a special assignment. They took off in the early morning, flew low level over Europe and dropped 4000 lb bombs into the mouths of vitally important railway tunnels. Each Mosquito crew had been given a tunnel to 'visit' and when the bomb had been dropped successfully the pilot would transmit his call sign and say 'Happy New Year' so that Ivor Broom could tick them off his list and keep a check on progress. The operation played havoc with the movement of German troops and ammunition. In places entire hillsides collapsed on to the railway tracks.

It so happened that Broom's wife Jessica had arrived that afternoon for a party in the mess so he was dismayed when Bennett rang and said "I want you to see something interesting on the photographs of your tunnel raids. Can you come to dinner tonight"? Broom explained that his wife was attending the mess party that evening so Bennett immediately invited her too. It was something of an honour for a young couple to be entertained at dinner by the AOC.

Behind Broom's Mosquito on the photographs was a German fighter which had been unable to catch him. Looking back some 40 years on to his days in Bennett's Light Night Striking Force Sir Ivor had this to say about this wartime chief:-

'If you were a professional in your job you got on with him like
a house on fire. If you were unprofessional he wouldn't let you
last five minutes.
I think he was the right man at the right time. And there is no
doubt that the Pathfinder Force as led by him made a great
contribution to the accuracy of the bombing offensive. He
couldn't stand bureaucracy. He is a 'doer' who wants to get on
with the job and he is very impatient with committees, or civil
servants, or ministers who want to take weeks and weeks in
reaching a decision when to him, it is all so simple — he can see
it all.
I've grown to like him in recent years as he has mellowed and
he has become a friend as opposed to the boss seeking high
standards. I had great admiration for him when I was very
young Acting Wing Commander.'

*   *   *   *

The Nuremberg raid of 30 March, 1944 must represent Bomber
Command's point of lowest fortune. It was a disaster.
According to Group Captain Mahaddie:-
'Nuremberg must be on Harris's heart. Because we should
never have gone. We had a little fellow called 'Titus' Oates of
the Mosquito Met Flight. He went over the whole route
backwards — way up to the Baltic, came down and then came
back. And he said "It is going to be gin clear. If there is going to
be any cloud it will be right over the target." '
Bennett was totally opposed to the raid as proposed by Harris
and for the first time there was near mutiny among the Squadron
Commanders, some of whom contacted Air Ministry direct with
a view to having the raid re-planned. Alec Thorn recalls that —
'Instead of using Pathfinder 'spoof' raids and 'doglegs' for
some reason a more direct route was taken. Bennett tried to
stop the raid but he was overruled. He said it would be suicide
— and it was. It was the worst night Bomber Command had
suffered.'
When the planned route, as misguidedly devised by H.Q.
Bomber Command, was sent to H.Q. Pathfinder Group Bennett
pressed to have it changed. However the Group Commanders
with Lancasters refused to support Bennett; they favoured a
direct route. Only AVM 'Roddy' Carr (AOC 4 Group which flew
Halifax bombers) and AVM C. M. McEwen (AOC 6 Canadian
Group) supported Bennett. In the event Harris refused to heed

the advice of his top navigation expert. It was his biggest mistake of the war — 545 aircrew died on that raid, another 200 were wounded and 159 were taken prisoner. Once again Bennett had been proved right. But this was an occasion when he would have been happier to have been wrong. In recent years he commented:-
'Everybody could see it was just pure suicide to go out on a clear, moonlight night, dead straight across Germany. You are not likely to get away with it. One of my bleats about warfare is that senior officers who don't know should be made to learn. It is as simple as that. In other words every senior officer should be required to operate. I would rather lose 10 AVMs than 10,000 airmen.'
Why did Arthur Harris press on with the Nuremberg raid when weather conditions were totally unsuitable and the tactics were wrong? Part of the trouble may lie with the fact that during their daylight raids the Americans had made exaggerated claims about the number of German fighters they were shooting down. In the confusion of battle this is quite understandable — the RAF was at times equally optimistic in its assessments. In fact German fighter strength was greater than Harris had been led to believe. Also, according to Air Vice-Marshal Saundby, Harris's SASO, Cochran had supported the raid. And in the eyes of the C-in-C Cochran was always right. Nuremberg was Harris's major miscalculation in an otherwise outstanding career.

*　　*　　*　　*

When, for any reason, a squadron was on stand-down in no time at all a mess party would be organised. So it was one night at Little Staughton where a dance was hurriedly arranged in the officer's mess. Don Bennett and his wife Ly would make every effort to look in and mix with those at the sharp end of war. He would drive like a thing possessed in his Hillman staff car — rumour has it that he reduced at least three of these vehicles to a heap of noisy tappets and body rattles.

'Hamish' Mahaddie often accompanied his chief on these occasions and towards the end of the evening he was approached by the station commander who was in a state of great agitation. He perspired somewhat freely as he told 'Hamish' out of the corner of his mouth that 'They've taken the wheels off Bennett's car and rolled them away into the night!'' 'Hamish' reminded the unfortunate Station Commander that the wheels on his own RAF issue car were the same as Bennett's and advised him to get

moving and make a swap, while he occupied the attention of the AOC Pathfinder Group. In Mahaddie's own words —
'I went up to a few Canadians and said "Mrs Bennett mustn't get off the dance floor — I'll explain later but keep her dancing — a big marathon — at least ten minutes." Of course she loved it. They were all cutting in on her. Meanwhile I went to the band and said "Not one beat must you miss until I tell you to rest." Bennett was standing in the entrance to the room and every time Ly came around he looked pointedly at his watch. She would say "Yes dear — I'm coming." Eventually the Station Commander gave the 'thumbs-up' sign — a set of wheels was back on the AOC's car.'

*   *   *   *

Geoffrey Leonard Cheshire had completed three tours of operations and not unnaturally the Air Ministry decided that he had done more than his share towards winning the war. So at the tender age of 25 they made him a Group Captain, then appointed him Station Commander of Marston Moor, an airfield situated between York and Harrogate, Yorkshire. It was not long before the young Group Captain realised that the life of a Station Commander was not for him. He desperately wanted to get back into flying.

'Bennett came for some reason. As he was getting ready to leave I went up to him and asked if he would have me in Pathfinder Force and he said "Well, I don't know. We'll have to test you and see if you are up to mark." Well you know how one is as a young fellow and I said he could keep it. But he made a terrific impression on me.'

Having regard to the fact that Cheshire had completed no less than three tours of operations Bennett's response to the young bombing ace's approach might be considered as rather less than forthcoming. However he felt, and indeed still feels, that although Cheshire was a gallant and able bomber pilot his specialist knowledge of navigation was no better than the average competent pilot of the day.

'Hamish' Mahaddie regards the Cheshire brush-off as one of Bennett's most misguided acts. Certainly he was to pay dearly for his momentary lack of tact on that occasion because Cheshire promptly joined 5 Group under AVM Cochran. There he disproved Don Bennett's firmly held belief that low level target marking in a metropolitan area was impractical. So it was in many cases. But Cheshire was given command of the famous 617 'Dam Buster' Squadron. He developed low-level formation techniques — three Lancasters flying tightly together at night, brushing the tree tops and often returning to base festooned with large branches or yards of telephone cable trailing behind. Cheshire found that by dive bombing the target, aiming his aircraft like a gun and then releasing the target indicator, he could mark the aiming point to an accuracy of 15 yards or so. Of course, low level marking was not practical against a heavily defended target; in that respect Cheshire fully agreed with Bennett.

'I've got full admiration for Bennett. But one should always make the exception. My argument is that the weakness of high level bombing in World War II is that you have got this long run in — so there is an inherent difficulty in the bombing technique. So, I was trying to argue ever since 1941, get around the difficulty by bringing in a different type of aircraft and going in low level. Furthermore it would disperse the defences; they have now got to get organised for low level attacks as well as high level.'

Word came through that Hitler was preparing a V3 weapon, a pump action gun that would pour shells into London at a high rate and force the British Government to evacuate the city. The gun was under 50 feet of reinforced concrete so in seeking ways of countering the threat the authorities enlisted the inventive genius of Barnes Wallis. He had previously evolved the special bombs that breached the Ruhr dams some months earlier. They called his 12,000 lb monster bomb Tallboy. It had a hard case which, when dropped from an aircraft, would penetrate 90 feet into the ground and, provided it could be positioned within 15 yards of the target, blow up the V3 gun from below.

Harris called a conference where he outlined the problem. Bennett made no bones about the task. Using current Pathfinder techniques he could not guarantee to place TIs within 15 yards of the target. Cheshire said he could achieve the required accuracy by using the low level techniques he had developed. Harris told him to work up 617 Squadron for the task. With Cochran's support they gradually reduced height at the point of release following a 30 degree dive. The V3 gun was destroyed.

As a result of this and other low level successes Harris removed a number of squadrons from Pathfinder Force and transferred them to 5 Group. Naturally Bennett was upset and a number of well-informed senior RAF officers of the period are of the opinion that this not only damaged Pathfinder Force; it was also to the disadvantage of Bomber Command as a whole because 5 Group began 'pathfinding' its own raids and this did not enhance standardisation. During his outstanding war career Cheshire was awarded a VC, three DSOs and a DFC.

*   *   *   *

Flying Officer J. Campbell and Flight Lieutenant A. Cleaver were over Stuttgart on the night of 21 November, 1944 when the 4000 lb bomb refused to drop from their Mosquito. A 'hang-up' was a rare but dreaded problem that occasionally had to be faced by bomber crews.

They made for Manston with its long, emergency runway and on landing the bomb dropped out then tumbled over the ground. The Mosquito ran about 100 yards before the bomb went off, wrecking the undercarriage and setting fire to the aircraft. Both crew members got out of the wreckage uninjured.

*   *   *   *

Late in April 1945 a force under the direction of a Master Bomber was sent to attack Hitler's so-called Eagle's Nest at Berchtesgarten. Group Captain Stafford Coulson, DSO, DFC, commander of 582 Squadron, had been led to believe that his unit would lead the raid. He had even picked the best crew for his Lancaster in anticipation and it was with some disappointment that he learned of changed plans; another squadron had been detailed for the job.

By that stage of the war German radar was rendered ineffective by Allied counter measures and the combined attention of the RAF and the US Air Force had so damaged German oil production capacity that the Luftwaffe was barely able to put up fighters. Against this background Stafford Coulson collected his crew and said "Come on chaps. We'll go straight there and come straight back." With that they filled his Lancaster with bombs and fuel while Coulson signed the authorisation sheet, giving his intentions as 'Ten hours navigation exercise.'

There was no opposition either during the run out or the flight home. The official bomber force had missed some parts of Berchtesgarten and Stafford had the satisfaction of plastering Hitler's house. His private war had been worthwhile.

He was greeted on his return by his adjutant who said "Air

Vice-Marshal Bennett was on the 'phone asking for you. He wanted you for a raid.'' ''What did you tell him''? asked a worried Coulson. ''I said you were on a ten hour navigation exercise and he was furious.''

Sequel to this little story is that in 1982 a reunion was held by 582 Squadron and the guests of honour were Don and Ly Bennett. After dinner Stafford Coulson got up and began a modest but not too serious account of his private bombing raid on Hitler's house, but after a few words Bennett said ''We don't wish to know that.'' After the laughter died down in the room it became clear that he had suspected what Coulson had done all those years ago.

*   *   *   *

Don Bennett's war came to a fairly abrupt end with events falling over one another at breakneck speed. Bomber Command cleared the Channel ports of Germans, destroyed rail communications and totally demoralised Von Runstedt's troops after their early success in mounting a counter offensive. The last operational sortie of the European war was flown by 125 Mosquitos of Bennett's Light Night Striking Force on 2 May 1945. It was a night raid against Kiel. Four days later Germany acknowledged defeat. Immediately Bomber Command became engaged in a massive airlift, bringing home prisoners of war. The first contingent was flown by Pathfinder Force with Don Bennett in command of the leading aircraft.

Plans had long been prepared for a bomber force which would join the Americans in attacking Japan and Bennett expected to take a leading part in these Pacific operations. For the task Avro had developed a bigger Lancaster which was called the Lincoln. However the atom bomb put an end to that and the Master Airman, still only 35 years of age, found himself confronted by a number of interesting possible careers, most of them outside the Royal Air Force, all of them offering new challenges.

Chapter 11
The Challenges of Peacetime

Those who have witnessed the event will know that the abrupt end of a major war involving half or more of the world's population is a remarkable experience. Obviously there is public euphoria in the victorious countries and at least a sense of relief among the war sick vanquished. But what of the great war machines that supplied the various fighting services? And what of the men and women in uniform?

It was not long after the collapse of Germany that America dropped two atom bombs on Japan. Whether or not it was right and proper to have delivered the second blow, or if it was indeed necessary, the use of this terrible weapon stopped the war and probably saved the lives of more than 500,000 Allied servicemen. There have been a number of post-war voices condemning the use of the atom bomb. No doubt these idealistically motivated people are sincere in their beliefs but they fail to recognise that the Pacific war was of Japan's choosing; it was forced upon an unwilling USA and an unprepared Britain. And it was in the nature of the Japanese nation to continue fighting long after their war was clearly lost.

Within weeks of VJ day, as the victory over Japan was named, plans were enacted for the rundown of armament production. In so far as the Royal Air Force was concerned flying ceased except for a limited amount of training, the movement about Europe of VIPs and essential officials and the repatriation of prisoners of war. Here and there odd incidents occurred, like the case of Werner Lindner, a pre-war Lufthansa captain who during the conflict served as a transport pilot in the Luftwaffe. The end of the war found him in Norway where he was captured and then screened along with other German prisoners. When the British found he was a very experienced pre-war German airline captain he was employed flying VIPs around Europe. They even made him an Honarary member of the Royal Air Force Association and he wears the badge with much pride to this day.

A system of release from service immediately came into effect. Service personnel were given a demobolisation code based upon age and number of years in uniform. Some elected to apply for a permanent commission while others, as yet uncertain about their civilian future, applied for a six or twelve month extension of their time in uniform.

Stopping the vast industrial machine making arms was another matter. One minute it is working day and night, turning out warships, tanks and aircraft. Then the entire global enterprise ceases even more suddenly than the enactment of Germany's invasion of Poland or Japan's unprovoked bombing of Pearl Harbour.

It was impossible to pull the switch on all these factories and send hundred of thousands of their staff home, with nothing to do. So the seemingly lunatic was a common sight up and down the country. For example, brand new Lancaster and Halifax bombers continued to leave the factories at a reduced rate. They would be flown to a number of airfields where gangs of men were paid to cut through the engine bearers with oxy-acetylene burners. Gleaming, factory-fresh Rolls-Royce Merlin and Bristol Hercules engines dropped to the ground while the remainder of these new aircraft was reduced to scrap.

By the time an end to the war was in sight many influential people within and outside RAF circles had formed the view that the still young Donald Bennett was rather more than an outstanding pilot and engineer. He had been proved right too often, usually in the face of concerted opposition from the other group commanders, for his talents to be ignored. It was this very talent for clear thinking that caused a ridiculous incident which should never have developed, one that resulted in his departing on a sour note the Royal Air Force he had served so well.

A number of people, including Harold Balfour, encouraged him to write a little booklet explaining his belief that world peace should in future be kept by an international police force. Bennett was still in uniform although within a matter of weeks he would be leaving the service. However he obtained permission from the Air Ministry before going into print. The day before publication he was sent for by the Chief of Air Staff, Air Chief Marshal Sir Charles F. A. Portal KCB, DSO, MC (later Marshal of the Royal Air Force Lord Portal). To his utter astonishment he was met with the words "I'd like you not to publish this book *(sic)* — it is quite the wrong policy for an Air Force officer to publish a book like this." In the first place the 'book' was no more than a booklet, secondly it had been cleared by the Air Ministry and was already in print and in any case Bennett was due to leave the RAF very shortly. Portal was not impressed with the facts. He continued "This will jeopardize you in my eyes — I am giving you an order not to publish." "Sir, you may give me the order" Bennett replied, "but I will publish and I will not be breaking any RAF legitimate order." At that stage Portal said "Bennett you are mad".

By general consent Portal was an outstanding man. 'Bomber' Harris described him as "marvellous — the best brain the Royal Air Force ever had" but this would seem to have been one of his less reasonable moments. Indeed, when not long after this painful interview Don Bennett was appointed first Chairman of the United Nations Association of Great Britain, Lord Portal joined him on the platform during a big meeting at the Albert Hall. It was an important occasion and the speakers were Clement Attlee, Lord Alexander, Anthony Eden, Eleanor Roosevelt and Don Bennett. However the booklet affair was pointless and a tragedy in so far as one of the most successful officers in the Royal Air Force left the service he loved with a feeling of deep resentment. Sir Archibald Sinclair, then Secretary of State for Air, had only recently asked Bennett to stand as unopposed Liberal Parliamentary candidate for Middlesbrough; he had toyed with the idea but the booklet now made up his mind. He walked out of Portal's office, down the corridor and through Sinclair's door. An MP he would be and the decision secured his immediate release from the RAF — a sad end to a distinguished career.

The transition from service to civilian life did not come easily to some. Five of their often most impressionable years had been spent in an organisation where the rank system, adequately labelled with appropriate badges of office, ensured that everyone knew their place, understood the limit of their powers and recognised the extent of their responsibilities. In this respect service life is far simpler than the cut and thrust of professional and commercial activities in the civil orbit. Those leaving the service were given a month of paid demobilisation leave and many of them returning to pre-war jobs, or perhaps a new career, could be seen wearing their uniforms until the last day. Of course, there were others who counted the hours before throwing away the old uniform and donning a 'demob' suit. But in Parliament newly elected members just out of the Navy, Army and Royal Air Force sat on the benches in their uniforms, among them Don Bennett resplendent in the light blue and gold braid of an Air Vice-Marshal.

Life in Westminster did not suit Don Bennett at all. He rapidly became disillusioned with the squalid little Parliamentary games being played at a time when Britain's shattered resources were in urgent need of re-building. Also he deeply resented the hostility towards Bomber Command, much of it emanating from left-wing politicians who later influenced the Attlee government into denying it the campaign medal it undoubtedly deserved — a festering sore that continues to this day.

Notwithstanding the pressures of running No. 8 Pathfinder Group in 1944 Don Bennett accepted the Deputy Mastership of the *Guild of Air Pilots and Air Navigators of the British Empire* (now a Livery Company of the City of London), an organisation founded in 1929 for the purpose of maintaining the highest of standards among professional air crew.

During the war most Guild members were flying with the services and the organisation was put into low gear under the caretakership of its Master, that great patron of aviation, The Marquis of Londonderry. Now the war was over and Don Bennett called a meeting of the Guild on 5 April, 1945. The report that followed promised regular Guild Journals, which in fact continue to this day, announced the formation of a Test Pilot Section and confirmed that the Air Ministry had asked the Guild's Panel of Examiners to resume testing civilian flying instructors and issuing Instructors' Certificates on its behalf (the writer had the honour of being Chairman of the Panel of Examiners from 1973 to 1983). The report ended in true, forthright, Bennett style.

"Our Civil Aviation has many faults and failings; destructive criticism and eternal bickering will not help. I suggest to you, therefore, with all due respect, that we just get on with the job."

Britain's first general election following the end of war in Europe swept the Labour party into power. Don Bennett lost his Middlesbrough seat and it was with some relief that he ceased to be an MP. But a new door was about to open.

Lord Beaverbrook was influential in the setting up of three national airlines after war. They would be known as British Overseas Airways Corporation, British European Airways and British South American Airways. Prior to this a group of shipping companies under the leadership of John Booth (of the

Booth Line) had formed a consortium with the intention of running an air service to the South Americas when peace returned. Member companies were Blue Star Line, Royal Mail, Lamport and Holt, Pacific Steam and Booth Line. £1,000,000 was subscribed to start the enterprise which they had originally decided to name British Latin American Airlines Ltd.

The intention was that BLAA would be run by shipping interests on a private enterprise basis (on the lines proposed by the Cadman Committee of 1938) and at the invitation of Lord Swinton, Bennett was invited to become managing director of the new airline. However when the Attlee government swept into power with a massive majority Swinton lost his seat and his place as a minister with responsibility for civil aviation was taken by Lord Winster. Labour policy was to nationalise every major activity in Britain and although Bennett resisted state take-over of BSAA it was all to no avail. Subsequent to his accepting the appointment at British South American Airways there were suggestions that Don Bennett might return home as Governor of Australia and while this would have suited him admirably, and probably saved him from a series of major crisis situations, he felt unable to let down Lord Swinton and the board of BSAA. But in the years to come there would be many an occasion when Don Bennett must have regretted turning down the possibility of a very important appointment in Australia which would have brought with it a Viscountcy.

From its inception BSAA generated antagonism from the two other airlines. BOAC in particular felt it had a claim on the South American routes, although some years later, when BOAC did fly to a number of countries in that continent the airline consistently lost money, blaming the British VC10 airliners for its own shortcomings. A private enterprise airline then took over the routes and made a profit with the same type of aircraft.

A meeting of the airlines was called with the Minister in the chair. BOAC was represented by its chairman, General Critchley, while John Booth and Don Bennett attended on behalf of BSAA. Critchley set about trying to impress the Minister with claims that BOAC could start flying the South American routes within three months. "And what can you do Bennett?" requested the Minister. Don Bennett told him that he had 12 Lancastrians, civil conversions of the wartime Lancaster bomber fitted with 13 comfortable, reclining seats. He also had more than forty ex-Pathfinder crews. At that stage Critchley accused Bennett of having nowhere to base his airline. He made clear there was no room for him at the BOAC base located on Hurn airport, near Bournemouth. "Surely you can spare one hangar for BSAA" protested the Minister whereupon Bennett told him not to worry since he had already made very satisfactory arrangements. His maintenance base had been set up at an airfield near the as yet undeveloped Heathrow Airport and it was under the direction of Group Captain Sarsby, ex-Chief Engineer of Pathfinder Force who knew every nut, bolt and rivet on a Lancaster. The Minister asked for the name of this airfield but Bennett replied "I would rather not tell you in front of Critchley; he would do anything he could to stop me."

After the meeting Bennett told the Minister that the Chairman of Wimpey, the big construction concern, was a fellow Australian. He had borrowed from him four small buildings at Heathrow, then in the process of becoming the main London Airport, and the use of the runway. Maintenance and hangarage were at nearby Langley Airfield which was owned by the manufacturers of the aircraft he was using. For obvious reasons they were glad to welcome and encourage BSAA.

The setting up of a new airline entails more than buying aircraft and employing suitable crews. Traffic has to be generated and tickets need to be sold. An early appointment to BSAA was Len Hough, ex-Imperial Airways and a traffic manager of great experience. Captain Gordon Store, the veteran airline pilot who had worked with Bennett during Imperial Airways days and who later helped him with the Atlantic Ferry, became Operations Manager. This very experienced South African airline captain had on a number of occasions flown Winston Churchill on important visits during the war. With so many ex-Pathfinder crews on the staff one might be excused for believing that BSAA could not have been in safer hands. For had not these crews flown Lancasters in the face of enemy action and through the European weather at a time when reliable forecasts were unobtainable? In the main events proved this assumption to be true. But not all of the flight deck crews represented the cream of Pathfinder talent; some had little flying experience and, in those days at any rate, the differing requirements of service flying and civil airline operations were not fully appreciated.

Although he is an Australian Bennett has always been more British than the average British in his patriotism and while the other state airlines fell over themselves in a scramble for American aircraft BSAA was happy with its Lancastrians. Certainly a civilian Lancaster carrying thirteen passengers instead of, say, a 20,000 pound bombload had plenty of power in reserve and if they were inclined to be noisy at least the type was well known to the ex-Pathfinder crews now flying them on BSAA routes. A less happy aircraft was another development of the Lancaster. It should be remembered that, by agreement with the USA, Britain's massive aircraft industry concentrated during the war on producing fighters and bombers while the Americans agreed to provide the Allies with transport aircraft, mainly Dakotas (DC3), four-engined Skymasters (DC4) and Constellations. At a late stage in the war the full implications of this arrangement, which gave the USA more than a head start on the air routes of the world when peace returned, must have come home to the British aviation authorities. Because Avro, builders of the Lancaster, received an order for a passenger aircraft using the wings, tail surfaces and other parts of the Lancaster. What emerged was the York, a high-wing monoplane that was very noisy and none too easy to fly. It could carry up to 30 passengers in a roomy cabin.

Don Bennett purchased his Lancastrians for only £30,000 each; the Yorks cost £40,000 but all of BSAA's aircraft were ex-RAF. With the assistance of the local ambassadors he also negotiated bi-lateral route agreements with the whole of Latin America except Mexico which was firmly under American influence.

The original route structure was Southampton — Lisbon — Bathurst — Natal — Rio de Janeiro — Montevideo. Later it was extended to Buenos Aires. Meanwhile a BOAC survey flight was started on 9 October 1945 with the legendary Captain O. P. Jones in command of Lancastrian G-AGMG. With him was Wing Commander B. T. Aikman. They left Hurn Airport (near Bournemouth) and visited all the places previously mentioned in addition to Santiago, Lima, Sal and Dakar. It was an attempt by that airline to pre-empt BSAAs activities.

BSAA's first proving flight departed Heathrow on 1 January 1946 with Don Bennett in command of Lancastrian *Star Light* (G-AGWG). This was, in fact, the first international departure from the new London Airport. The new airline had to face competition on the routes from eight other airlines but at least it was in business.

Initially BSAA was a very small airline with only 12 captains and 15 first officers, most of them ex-Pathfinder Force. All the aircraft were given names beginning with the word 'Star' and the stewardesses were known as 'Stargirls'. Early flights to Buenos

Aires took all of twenty-four hours. There were no crew changes — such periods on duty would never be allowed today by any airline. In 1946 it was considered quite normal.

Joan Thompson (later Joan Forbes) became Senior Stargirl with BSAA. She well remembers the electrically charged atmosphere with the little airline:-

"It was terrific — it was absolutely marvellous. I enjoyed every minute of it although we had some sad moments and lost a lot of good friends."

Of the three British State airlines BSAA had the toughest routes; they entailed some of the longest water crossings in the world and, having reached South America great mountain ranges had to be overflown; they blocked out radio communications during most of those parts of the routes. Then some of the airfields needed for refuelling stops were, to say the least, primitive. Radio aids were crude, even in Europe but particularly so on the South American routes. In any case most of the modern navigational aids that even light 'plane pilots now accept as a minimum requirement had yet to be invented.

Although the Lancastrians and Yorks were considered by Bennett to be safer than contemporary aircraft from the USA BSAA was plagued by a series of accidents, many of them minor, others serious. The worst of these was the loss of Lancastrian *Star Dust* (G-AGWH) which on 2 August 1947 disappeared in the Andes. Some years later an Indian from Chile was spotted wearing an aircrew-type wristwatch. When questioned he said he had found it on a skeleton in a wrecked aircraft. It was no figment of his imagination; later the man led a search party to the wreckage of *Star Dust* and it was found to have been several hundred miles off track when it flew into the mountain top. The following month another Lancastrian, *Star Trail*, arrived over Bermuda in a thunderstorm at night, circled for some time in the hope that it would move away until shortage of fuel forced the crew to attempt a landing. At 300 feet they were still in cloud and descending when the aircraft struck an aerial. Fortunately no one was hurt. In October of that year another BSAA aircraft crashed at London Airport and the following month Lancastrian *Star Light* (G-AGWG) bit the dust while making a night landing at Bermuda with one of its four engines failed. Fortunately there were no injuries in either of these accidents but every time BSAA suffered an incident of this kind BOAC used it to support their claim on the South American routes. Only when that airline suffered its own accidents did it stop pointing the finger at BSAA.

In fairness to both airlines it should be remembered that these were the immediate post war years, aircraft were not as reliable then as, for example, modern jets and turboprops, radio aids were few and operating experience was being gained the hard way.

Part of BSAA's trouble could have been that its RAF trained crews were yet to appreciate that what might be right and proper in the course of military flying could be totally unacceptable in the civil airline environment. Don Bennett, with past experience as an Imperial Airways Captain, recognised the problem and devoted considerable time to urging his ex-Pathfinder boys along other alleys. But it seems clear that he did not always support his Operations Manager, Gordon Store.

Store was a totally different type of man to Bennett. The ex-Pathfinder chief was (and remains) a quick thinking, swift acting person, totally confident in hs own judgement which is very often right. Store, on the other hand, is a solid, deliberate plodder. The more assertive and fast-acting might regard him as dyed-in-the-wool and so forth but the fact remains that this very distinguised airline captain had flown the routes of the world, often carrying world leaders, and he had an outstanding record of safety. Gordon Store did things by the book. He wanted simulator and instrument training — the idea was not popular among the ex-Pathfinder crews. He pressed for the use of checklists but experienced resistance from some of the wartime pilots. While aircraft remained simple such rituals as the pre-take off and pre-landing vital actions (relating to setting up the various controls) could be recited off the back of one's head, using easy to remember mnemonics. But aircraft have always tended to become more and more complicated and the checklist has assumed a vital role in modern flying. Don Bennett gave qualified support for checklists; he had managed without them for years and aircraft were still relatively simple. However, Store admits that "Bennett had a talent for generating loyalty. To the sixty or so ex-Pathfinder pilots who joined BSAA he was "like God in their eyes."

Ex-Senior Stargirl Joan Forbes remembers an amusing checklist related incident when Don Bennett was arriving at Heathrow in a Lancastrian at the end of a proving flight. It was the fashion in those days to display a little company flag on a short mast attached above one of the flightdeck windows. Before take-off it was brought inside but on this occasion no checklist had been used and the first officer had great difficulty retrieving

In its day the Tudor cabin set new standards of comfort.

The Fairtravel 'Linnett', one of seven built by Don Bennett's company before competition from a government-subsidised concern forced him to cease production.

Fairthorpe 'Electron Minor' sports cars at the Valencia Motor Show.

Don and Ly Bennett taking part in the 1959 Monte Carlo Rally in a Fairthorpe car of their own manufacture.

Don Bennett's private Heathrow was no little airstrip (Blackbushe Airport as seen from the air).

Ly Bennett with son Torix and daughter Noreen.

Air Vice Marshal Donald Bennett CB., CBE., DSO., FRAeS and Ly Bennett at the 1984 Pathfinder Ball held at the Savoy Hotel, London.

the flag before landing. Don Bennett was determined not to arrive before the reception party with a flag shredded by the airflow.

Another view of British South American Airways is expressed by Group Captain Geoffrey H. Womersley DSO, DFC, a wartime Pathfinder who had studied to become an airline pilot during the late 1930s. After the war he flew for BSAA, eventually as Chief Pilot.

"I think Bennett was rather disappointed that more had not joined him at BSAA from Pathfinder Force. I remember when it was announced that he was going to BSAA he came round and asked people to find out if anyone on their station wanted to join him. I wrote a note to all the pilots on my station asking anyone who was interested to come and see me. I was absolutely staggered that only one man did although some wanted to stop in the RAF if they could."

Womersley remembers that everyone at BSAA was very concerned about the accidents although he is adamant that most of them were not caused by ex-Pathfinder pilots.

"I think Bennett wanted to have half a dozen or more ex-BOAC captains to start the airline. The rest of us would go out under their supervision for several trips. This didn't happen and the only two who joined him were Gordon Store and David Brice. Some of the people — this is my opinion — put up for command had very little experience. A lot of them had never taken-off a heavy bomber. I think you will find that most of the people involved in these accidents were those people."

According to Womersley some of the pilots had only 1000 hours flying experience, however while this left BSAA open to criticism it should be remembered that these were immediate post-war days and during the war young men were flying heavy bombers on operational duties with little more than 300 hours in their logbooks. But the checklist controversy should have been settled by Don Bennett one way or another, preferably by supporting the BSAA Operations Manager. Womersley recalls-

"We had always in the Royal Air Force used nmemonics. There was a lot of opposition to bringing in checklists. In fact, I was sent out to relieve one captain who had flatly told Gordon Store that he would not use a checklist. My view was that a checklist probably had its uses and as aircraft were going to get more and more complicated we were going to have to use them."

All of us, however brilliant, are possessed of our own pet prejudices. Don Bennett certainly has his own likes and dislikes, however Womersley describes his old chief thus—

"Technically he was a genius. No man I ever met knows as much about aviation, navigation, radio, radar or maintenance of aircraft. He had this total tenacity in Pathfinder Force. All he thought about was winning the war. I never remembered him taking a holiday."

Gordon Store describes Bennett as being "violently pro-British; rather anti-American" and this sometimes caused him to reject equipment which would have been of benefit to the airline. Store wanted to use the Radio Compass. Bennett favoured an old-fashioned two-finger instrument which would not provide a clear 'over-the-beacon' indication.

To his credit Bennett ran BSAA at a profit from the moment it started operating. The other state airlines, on the other hand, were grossly overstaffed, a problem that was finally solved in 1980 by merging Overseas and European divisions under a tough chairman. But BSAA's profit made heavy demands on the cabin staff. What was it like to be a Stargirl in 1946? According to Joan Forbes:-

"We worked terribly hard and did far more hours than the other airlines (where BOAC needed 100 staff, BSAA had only 17). We doubled up on all sorts of things. For instance Stargirls, when they weren't flying, did passenger reception at the airport."

BSAA used to receive applications for Stargirl jobs by the hundred. Joan Forbes made a short list and they were interviewed by a board on which Bennett usually sat. Was the job worth it?

"It was very badly paid — they got £4 a week, when they started, for speaking two or three languages. Some of them had nursing training. We were allowed to have £5 in the currency of every country we flew through. It was deducted from your wages. And in the whole time I was with them I only got one salary cheque — that was the first one. After that I always owed them money because I had overdrawn my wages going down the line.

But we used to do everybody's shopping for them. We made a bit of profit on the things we brought back — pineapples for the Savoy, nylon stockings, crocodile handbags — all that sort of thing."

Discussing BSAA with ex-pilots and cabin crews a clear

picture emerges of 'Pathfinder' Bennett attempting a repeat performance with his civil airline. Indeed one hears such comments as "Bennett tried to run BSAA like the Air Force" and "He was marvellous on the aircraft side but the passengers were purely coincidental." While Bennett was admired almost without exception his serious approach to life did not endear him to the staff. But theirs was not the responsibility of making the airline succeed and after the hard years of war there was a tendency in Britain for even quite senior employees to covert the easy life.

"He was so different from the rest of us. We all enjoyed life; we had a lot of fun; we all had a tremendous sense of humour — got on like a house on fire. We all went down to the pub and had a drink — went dancing — we all smoked. He didn't drink. He didn't smoke. And I don't think he approved of us doing so. When we weren't flying we really enjoyed life. He wasn't the sort of person you could let your hair down with."

On one occasion when Bennett made a proving flight to Venezuela the crew were entertained rather lavishly to rum punch at a reception held by the government. The First Officer and one of the Stargirls managed to over-indulge themselves, Don Bennett arrived and virtually sent them to bed like naughty children.

Catering was handled under contract by Lyons. They called it 'Frood' — cooked and then frozen before going into the aircraft's oven for reheating in flight. The menu was more restricted in those days than it is now but they managed a main course and a sweet followed by cheese, a lot of the meal passed around the cabin by Stargirls.

One of BSAA's destinations was Rio de Janeiro where the international airport is built on Governor's Island. Today it is linked to the city by a long causeway; in those days it was not and the shipping interests within the airline provided passengers with a launch. When they pulled out of the airline and wanted to make a charge for the service Bennett decided to buy a company launch and the craft, more than 100 feet long, was delivered at Tower Steps, London where they named it *Star Haven*. Bennett planned to navigate it out to Rio along with his chairman who was a Master Mariner but, knowing the magnitude of the task, the old salt opted out leaving Don Bennett to find his own crew.

They got no further than the Bay of Biscay before fuel feed problems and sea sickness defeated the crew and they brought *Star Haven* back to England where it was eventually sold to a firm conducting pleasure trips.

It was the introduction of a new airliner that sowed the seeds of BSAA's demise. Under the Attlee government civil airliners were ordered by the civil servants, more or less without reference to BOAC, BEA or BSAA. The airline would then be told to operate them. A more lunatic arrangement than this would be hard to conceive but when Avro produced the Tudor, a new generation airliner with a pressurised cabin, it was so down on performance that BOAC virtually refused to accept delivery. However aircraft are capable of provoking emotions of love or intense hatred among flying men and if to BOAC the Tudor was an object of revulsion Don Bennett saw it very differently. It was from Avro, the firm who during the war had built his magnificent Lancasters, it was British and Roy Chadwick, its designer, he regarded as the best in the world. BSAA would operate the Tudor, wave the flag with a British airliner and at the same time get off the hook the civil servants who now found themselves with egg on their faces and a rebellious BOAC.

Not everyone shared Don Bennett's enthusiasm for the Tudor at BSAA. According to Gordon Store:-

"The Tudor was built like a battleship, it was noisy, I had no confidence in its engines and its systems were hopeless. The Americans were 50 years ahead of us in systems engineering. All the hydraulics, the air conditioning equipment and the re-circling fans were crammed together underneath the floor without any thought. There were fuel-burning heaters that would never work and we had the floor boards up in flight again and again."

In general the cabin staff did not like the Tudor. The galley was at the rear of the aircraft and in rough weather the tail would gyrate in all directions, although some modern airliners are so inclined. At times passengers and crew alike froze in that aircraft. On the other hand Captain Geoffrey Womersley, who eventually became Chief Pilot of BSAA, felt rather differently about the Tudor.

"I thought at that time it was the best civil airliner flying. The troublesome heater was later fitted to the Canadair and it worked perfectly."

Nevertheless the heater was regarded with rather less than affection, even by Womersley. On one occasion he was on the way from Bermuda and nearing London. During the descent there was a colossal flash!

"The next thing I knew there were three of us standing around the heater with fire extinguishers. We all thought the heater had blown up but it was nothing to do with that — it was one of those static discharges. The passengers reported seeing it pass right down the cabin. We found where the discharge had occurred."

Of course these were the days before weather radar, yet the Tudor was being flown at heights where it could easily enter a thunderstorm buried within a layer of cloud. But even when some years later the Comet was introduced it was operated with basic equipment of a kind that would be totally unacceptable in a modern light aeroplane today. Like all activities, aviation learns with experience.

The Tudor was to destroy British South American Airways and cost Don Bennett his job. During January 1948 Tudor G-AHNP, *Star Tiger* disappeared without trace while approaching Bermuda. A year later after Bennett had left the airline, G-AGRE, *Star Ariel* took off from Bermuda and climbed to 20,000 feet. It reported established at its cruising level and was never heard of again.

Why did BSAA lose two Tudors? Don Bennett is adamant that both airliners were sabotaged on the orders of those who felt threatened by the possibility of a successful challenge to their interests. He will tell you that in the case of *Star Tiger,* first of the two aircraft to be lost, a known war-registered saboteur was seen standing nearby shortly before it left Santa Maria in the Azores for Bermuda on its last flight, that with the aid of Air Commodore Pointer (head of MA5 who knew the names of those involved) he was getting uncomfortably close to the truth in his enquiries when Prime Minister Attlee gave instruction for the matter to be dropped because of the effect such findings might have on international relations. It has not been possible to find any real support for these views and since the accident investigations were unsuccessful in producing any conclusive reasons of either accident we are left with speculation.

Captain Womersley does not entirely rule out the possibility of sabotage but thinks it more likely that a propeller broke away, cut through the fuselage and severed the control cables. A similar propeller had been known to depart its engine on other occasions. He regarded the flight from the Azores to Bermuda as a very demanding exercise because, in those days, there were no navigational aids until the last 200 miles or so and much depended on astro techniques. Captain Gordon Store feels that the second crash was caused by failure of a high pressure hydraulic line causing fumes which were circulated through the air conditioning but *Star Tiger,* he believes, probably flew into the sea at night.

The Ministry of Civil Aviation of the day published an accident report on *Star Tiger.* It is dated September 1948 and having studied its contents the author is inclined to agree with Captain Store. Some interesting facts emerge and these should have received more consideration. The flight started badly with the usual cabin heater trouble between London and Lisbon, some engine problems and a fault in the gyro compass system. Consequently, departure from Lisbon to the Azores was two and a half hours late. There were strong headwinds across the South Atlantic and the Tudor captain discussed these with the commander of a BSAA Lancastrian that was on a freight run, also to Bermuda. Both pilots agreed to delay the next part of the flight until the wind dropped so there was an unscheduled night stop.

At 15.34 on the afternoon of Thursday 29 January, 1948 *Star Tiger* with its captain, first officer, navigator, radio operator, two Stargirls and twenty-five passengers took off from Santa Maria for the 1960 nautical mile sea crossing to Bermuda. Normally a Tudor would have flown at 20,000 feet or so, however, although they had abated slightly there were still persistent headwinds and it was decided to make the trip at only 2000 feet where the winds were lighter. The Lancastrian went on ahead, its captain reporting back good weather. At half-hourly intervals the Tudor's radio operator sent back position reports on his morse transmitter and it is an astonishing feature of these reports that although *Star Tiger* had flight planned to fly at 2000 feet every message from the aircraft mentioned 20,000 feet. The flight continued until 3.15 a.m. the following morning when *Star Tiger* obtained a radio bearing from Bermuda. It was acknowledged immediately. That was the last message to be sent by the aircraft. What sudden disaster struck the Tudor? Two factors seem important. First, the headwinds were stronger than anticipated and *Star Tiger* was in fact about 30 minutes further from its destination than the captain believed — this was later checked by calculating the effects of the wind. Then there was the constant reporting of *Star Tiger's* cruising altitude as 20,000 feet instead of 2000 feet. Imagine the situation on that flight deck. The crew imagine they are nearing Bermuda with 20,000 feet of height to lose. So they start to go down and, after descending through only 2000 feet, hit the sea in the dark, the aircraft disintegrates on impact and is lost without trace. Would an experienced captain make such a fundamental mistake? This explanation may sound too simple to be true yet the altimeters of those days, which relied on three fingers with a very small one indicating heights in tens of thousands of feet, could be misread. 2000 feet could be mistaken for 20,000 feet, particularly if you were tired and hard pressed. In fact this captain, who had been under stress since leaving London, having to deal with one problem after another, was known to have complained of feeling very tired while at Santa Maria.

Whatever the reason for the loss of *Star Tiger* it was the beginning of the end for Don Bennett. He was sent for by Lord Nathan, Minister of Civil Aviation, and told to ground the Tudors. Bennett made it clear that he had no justification for doing this, particularly as the Air Registration Board had refused to remove their Certificate of Airworthiness. "Then I will do it myself" replied the Minister.

One day in February, 1948 the *Daily Express* carried an exclusive interview, written by Basil Cardew of that newspaper under a bold heading which proclaimed "I CONTEST LORD NATHAN'S GROUNDING OF TUDOR IV by Air Vice-Marshal D. C. T. Bennett." In it he complained of " — those who are openly anti-British in aviation." He also derided people who entered aviation for their own selfish reasons but who remained totally ignorant of aviation. He rightly drew attention to interference with airline management, the outrageous aircraft ordering system that had been devised by politicians and civil servants and the unreasonable demand he had received from the Minister of Civil Aviation who wanted him to ground the Tudor. He made it clear that he had the utmost confidence in that aircraft and resented the fact that aviation had become a political football.

There was much in that newspaper interview with which it is hard to disagree. But it was strong stuff and Lord Nathan could not have cared for it. Eventually Don Bennett was sacked, solely because of his refusal to ground the Tudor fleet. By this time Captain Womersley was Chief Pilot of BSAA and he remembers Bennett telling him "Never resign Geoff. Always make them sack you".

Air Commodore Brackley, ex-Imperial Airways and at the time one of the most experienced Operations Directors in the world, took over from Don Bennett. Tragically he was drowned soon afterwards in Rio. Then there was the second Tudor loss and that left BSAA without any modern aircraft to fly. It was the end of the road and the airline's interests were merged with BOAC. But it was certainly not the end of the road for the Master Airman and he was soon to prove that, despite Lord Nathan's fears, the Tudor could do a job of work.

Chapter 12
Going it alone

It could, perhaps with some justification, be claimed that Bennett's accomplishments as chief executive of the British South American Airways Corporation were not to be compared with his outstanding leadership of Pathfinder Force. True there were too many accidents, although most of them were not of a serious nature. But on the other side of the achievement balance sheet was the fact that he operated the airline at a profit while the other state carriers were a drain on the tax-paying public. Then there was his stubborn insistence on buying British aircraft. Since the war it has become unfashionable for the British to exhibit outward signs of patriotism. Of course, an excess of patriotic fervour can lead to a situation such as that orchestrated in Hitler's Germany up to and during the war. But if such excesses have proved to be the detriment of mankind it could surely be argued that the other extreme can, if not challenged from time to time, destroy the confidence and will to succeed of a nation. In this respect there were no doubts in Bennett's mind. Britain had built some of the finest commercial flying boats before the war, during the conflict its massive aircraft industry had produced the unmatchable Mosquito, the very successful Hurricane and Spitfire and no fewer than three successful heavy bombers, including the outstanding Lancaster. By contrast, for all their technical merit, and notwithstanding the fact that they had been preparing for war over a period of many years, the German aircraft industry failed to produce a single practical heavy bomber. So when the Tudor arrived he was determined to make it a success. And if it had a number of shortcomings he would iron out the problems in the light of operating experience.

It is rare indeed that a totally new transport aircraft is without its problems. But with experience these often quite minor faults are recognised, isolated and cured by the manufacturers. The fact that in producing an excellent aircraft even the best manufacturer can rarely 'hole in one' is something the Americans have known for many years. The British, on the other hand, only realised the fact some quarter century after the war end.

Lord Nathan, Minister of Civil Aviation, must have been very concerned about the loss of *Star Tiger*. But the Tudor was not the first new airliner to crash; the Americans have on a number of occasions faced similar setbacks yet they did not over-react, remove the Certificate of Airworthiness and ground all aircraft of the type. So in resisting the Minister's demands to ground the Tudor, Bennett was, as usual, acting from a position of cold logic based upon his superb knowledge of the subject. Nathan, on the other hand, was over-reacting from emotion. Had Don Bennett played his hand differently the Tudor affair might have ended on a different note. It may even have gone on to make BSAA's fortune. For did not the ill-fated Comet of some years later arise from the ashes in improved and modified form to give an excellent account of itself in RAF and airline service? Indeed a military variant of the Comet, in essence based closely on the original aircraft, remains in service up to date of this publication, and seems likely to continue for many years, although the original design first flew in July 1949. Such opinions as these, that Lord Nathan was wrong when he grounded the Tudor and that he would have been wise to have accepted the expert advice of those appointed to run the airline were, in any case, soon to be proved by Bennett.

When he was dismissed from BSAA Don Bennett had no income other than a few quite small fees earned in the course of advising foreign airlines. He was out of a job for six months when a conflict between former friends presented him with the type of challenge that appealed to his get-up-and-go nature. Russia closed the access road to West Berlin in the hope that the soft and timid West would hand over the city with no more than feeble words of indignation. What happened next surprised the world, not least the Kremlin.

The panic was on to supply Berlin by air. At first the RAF and the American Air Force organised an endless air shuttle but it rapidly became clear that, on their own, they would not be capable of feeding West Berliners. There was also a need for oil, coal and consumer supplies such as clothes, household goods and so forth.

The authorities started casting around for more capacity. Naturally it was to the various independent operators that they turned and Bennett immediately set about forming his own air freight company. By now the Labour Government had been replaced, Lord Nathan was no longer Minister of Civil Aviation and his place was taken by Peter Thorneycroft who was no stranger to Bennett. "Sell me some Tudors and I will help the Berlin Airlift" he told the Minister. It so happens that there were standing idle a few enlarged versions of the Tudor that had been stretched to increase their passenger-carrying capacity. However, in the light of Lord Nathan's grounding of the type they had remained unfurnished and there was no pressurisation. But they would make ideal freighters for the Berlin Airlift. Such an enterprise entailed great financial risks so he discussed the project with his wife. Ly took it all in and said "If that is what you want to do, I am with you all the way".

Don Bennett went to the City of London and raised money for his Tudors. Then he formed a new company, Airflight Ltd, based it at Langley, the Avro airfield not far from London, and ran the operation from his home set in fourteen acres of beautiful gardens. Bennett's detractors will often tell you he was unpopular with his staff yet the ink was barely dry on the new company's articles of association before Eileen Gummer, his ex-secretary from BSAA, arrived on the doorstep and said "I'm coming in." She was to run the airline's administration under Ly Bennett who was a director of the company. The airline was managed from the Bennett's home. And he was also joined by Sarsby, ex-chief engineer of Pathfinder Force and BSAA.

Initially much of the flying was done by Don Bennett and, for the first five months, all of the night flying. He did not exactly spare himself.

Flying many trips with full loads over a short period the aircraft rapidly paid for themselves. In fact after only one year they owed him nothing and Bennett had enough money put by to start new enterprises. But life on the Berlin Airlift was not without its moments of drama. It should be realised that in the late 1940s and early 1950s radio aids were still rather primitive yet a great number of aircraft, civil and military, flew into and out of Berlin's airfields, often in the most appalling weather. One night, when the visibility was below limits, Bennett and his Tudor crew were waiting impatiently for permission to take off. After a while Bennett rushed out of the met office, clambered aboard the aircraft and as the flight engineer shut the door he shouted "Everything OK — you've done everything?" (a reference to the pre-flight external and internal checks) to which the engineer affirmed.

Up on the flight deck the first officer was already settled into the right-hand seat. They started the engines, taxied out in the murk, and Bennett ran through the pre-take-off vital actions. These included a 'full and free movement of the controls' check to ensure that nothing was jamming them and that the autopilot was disengaged. Not long after lift-off Bennett was dismayed to find that he could not move the elevator control — it was locked solid. An emergency was declared over the radio.

The aircraft was almost unmanageable, the weather was foul and it was difficult to locate the runway. In an effort to find it Bennett made four circuits of the airfield at only 200 feet as, with great skill, he adjusted speed and pitch attitude on the throttles. It was a situation guaranteed to maintain the blood pressure and concentrate the mind.

A lesser pilot than the Master Airman would have given up the struggle and perhaps crashed the big aircraft in a built-up area with terrifying consequences. In the event, the airfield lights appeared out of the gloom and he made a respectable landing which nevertheless used up almost every inch of the runway. It had been a remarkable performance, one that more than ever confirmed Don Bennett's high opinion of the Tudor.

What had happened? To prevent damage to the flying controls (elevators, ailerons and rudder) while the aircraft is parked on the ground control locks are fitted to prevent them being blown about by the wind. In those days control locks took the form of external clamps, usually fitted with long, red streamers to remind those carrying out the pre-flight checks that they must be removed. On this occasion the flight engineer had not completely removed the elevator clamps and as Bennett made the take-off they snapped back into position. That incident more than ever convinced Don Bennett that the Tudor had a lot going for it. Many aircraft would have proved unflyable under similar circumstances.

Airflight's Tudors made a big contribution to the Berlin Airlift. They could fly in the best part of ten tons and were probably the best weight-lifters at the time. The combined effort of all involved in this historic operation was such that some two-and-a-half million West Berliners were supplied, from 26 June, 1948 when the Berlin Airlift first started and for the next twelve months by which time the Russians were forced to acknowledge the failure of their plans. It was the biggest airlift in history with a constant stream of aircraft arriving and departing at all hours of the day and night. Wünstorf and Gatow handled traffic for Berlin in addition to Tegel in the French sector while the Americans used Tempelhof. Over at Hamburg the airport of Fuhlsbuttel also shared traffic. All manner of aircraft could be seen at these airfields; RAF Yorks and Hastings, more Yorks from Skyways Ltd, Lancastrians from Flight Refuelling Ltd (Sir Alan Cobham's famous company), Bristol Freighters belonging to Silver City Ltd, others from Airwork and, biggest of them all, the Tudors of Airflight Ltd.

Operators of four-engined aircraft were paid £70 per flying hour and the government supplied all petrol and maintenance. In those days £70 was a lot of money. So successful was the operation that eventually the Airlift had sufficient capacity to fly in non-essential luxury goods. The operation was run from Schloss Bückeburg, once a royal residence.

When the futility of further antagonising their ex-allies finally percolated into the Kremlin, Russia honoured its end-of-war agreements and opened the road to Berlin. The Airlift was over. By then Airflight had a healthy bank balance and Don Bennett was tempted to sell the company as a going concern. The deal was completed, then the new owner said he did not really want the aircraft — he was only interested in acquiring the bank balance. So Don Bennett found himself the owner of his two Tudors and they were to form the basis of his new company, Fairflight Ltd. Whereas Airflight had specialised in carrying bulk freight, Fairflight was to transport people, some of them under extraordinary circumstances.

There were some flights to Korea during the war between North and South. Then the aircraft were chartered to fly Moslems on the Hadj pilgrimage. But one of the more remarkable assignments handled by Fairflight occurred not long after the war that followed the establishment of the State of Israel. The company flew many trips ferrying Jews from the Yemen to the new state. For these people nothing had changed in several thousand years. Electricity was unknown yet the aeroplane was accepted quite naturally. Because had not the Old Testament told them

'--- Prepare ye the way of the Lord, make straight in the desert a highway for our God ', and '--- they shall mount up with wings as eagles'. *(Isaiah, Ch. XL, verses 3 and 31).*

And here it was, Don Bennett's Eagle, waiting to take them out of a desert slavery to the Promised Land. So under-nourished and tiny were these people that 142 could be carried in a Tudor which normally seated 78 passengers. What was it like to fly a cabin full of people who belonged to the age of oil lamps and the crudest of existence? According to Don Bennett:-

"They were Jews in an Arab land. They had been starved for years, in fact generations. They were more or less slaves. We would put them in a seat and they would slide on to the floor — they didn't want to sit on a seat. The first flights were terrible — they lit fires on the floor! It was not that they were cold. It was just habit."

Like the Berlin Airlift all manner of small charter companies were flying people into Israel. For example there was Near East Airlines, an outfit operating four-engined DC4 aircraft. They too were flying in refugees from the Yemen. These were hectic days and the crews worked long hours. One such was Johnnie Jacobs, an ex-RAF navigator, now flying with Near East Airlines. He was in the airport bar at Lydda, tired and thirsty after a nine-hour flight in the heat, much of it requiring the use of astro navigation. His Mk 9A sextant was on the table near a collection of full glasses and empty bottles when he became aware that a stranger was taking some interest in the instrument. "Do you know anything about navigation?" he asked and the stranger replied, "Yes, but I don't like these." "Well, what do you like?" countered a slightly irritated Johnnie and the stranger replied "I prefer the old Mk 8." At this stage of the conversation Johnnie Jacobs felt moved to deliver the stranger a lecture on air navigation in tones that left no room for discussion or a dissenting view.

Back at the table with his American crew mates one of the pilots looked up at Johnnie and asked "What had Bennett got to say?" Good God" he replied, his face going red, "that wasn't Bennett was it?"

It was while Don Bennett was out of the country that Fairflight accepted a charter which on 12 March, 1950 ended in a disaster of such magnitude that it discouraged him from continuing operations. It would have discouraged any man. The Tudor involved was G-AKBY, the one he had successfully landed that dark and wet Berlin night when the elevator locks had re-engaged themselves. He said of the accident:-

"That was the one black mark against the Tudor — the only one. Here again, I cannot be certain but although there was an investigation I believe they kept one piece of evidence from me. I wasn't here in the country at the time but we took a charter flight with Dennis Parsons as captain and went off with a full load of football fans from Cardiff to Dublin. On the way back they were coming in to land at Llandow [near Cardiff] when for no apparent reason the nose went up and the aircraft stalled. All but a few people were killed. I rushed there. I was not allowed to see the wreckage — after all I was only the owner of it — but it was very strictly under the accident investigation people. So I bided my time and was not allowed to see anything until they had finished, and then without much co-operation, I did a lot of tests; there was some suggestion that the centre of gravity was too far aft and so I did a flight, with an Air Registration Board man, with the C. of G. twelve inches outside the aft limit. There was adequate elevator control — no problem at all. So we were at a loss to know why it had happened.

We had the enquiry with every QC in the country raking in his thousands of guineas for five minutes talk, displaying ignorance that was unbelievable. They hadn't the faintest notion which end of an aeroplane went first.

This went on for a week or ten days while they all raked in the money. So far as I was concerned it all remained a mystery.

Six months later I was at Avro's Woodford and they said 'Oh yes, this is the bolt that failed.' They showed me that the elevator hinge was the same as on the Lincoln. On the Lincoln they had had failures — people over-tightening, the hinge then collapsed and elevator control was lost. That was never mentioned in the enquiry."

Discussing the tragedy some thirty-four years later Don Bennett was firmly of the view that, being such a stable aircraft by nature, the only possible cause of the sudden pitch up while coming in to land would be failure of an elevator hinge and the consequent loss of control in the pitching plane. Although he discussed the matter with the various authorities they seemed unable to admit the possibility of a fundamental design fault, something that would have reflected badly on those responsible for certificating the Tudor in the first instance. However, recent enquiries at the old Avro factory (which is now part of British Aerospace) reveal that the same bolts were used on the Lancaster and Lincoln bombers, the civil Tudor and the Shackleton maritime patrol aircraft, some of which are still flying in 1985. These bolts have never been modified so it seems that Don Bennett could have been misinformed, unless a bolt had been over-tightened.

Whatever the reason for the disaster Don Bennett decided to cease operation and devote his talents and energies to other things. Immediately after the Berlin Airlift he had set up a small engineering works making parts as subcontractors to the aircraft industry. Work came in from many quarters until in 1951 there was a change of policy at Ministry level, subcontracting was frowned upon and within a few weeks they had no orders. Meanwhile there were twenty or so highly skilled machinists to pay. Most people faced with a situation of this kind would have looked around other industries and offered to make bits for washing machines, bicycles, nuts and bolts or suchlike. Not Don Bennett. "We will design and build our own cars," he announced with a certainty born of an unquestioned belief that they would do just that.

Within three weeks he had designed and built the first car, the Fairthorpe Electron. The cheapest model, called Atom 1, had a 250 cc BSA motorcycle engine. The original model gave a new dimension to the word 'slow' but it traded speed for economy and returned a then staggering 60 miles per gallon. There were also Atom 2 and Atom 3 versions with more powerful engines and an Electron sports car which went like the wind under the urgings of the highly acclaimed Coventry Climax engine. The first example was entered in eight American sports car races and managed to win seven of them.

There was also Electron Minor which Fairthorpe offered with a choice of hotted-up Ford or Triumph 1100 engines and this became their main production model. Attractive fibreglass bodies were designed for the cars by Ken Low, founder and owner of the well known Kenlow motor accessory firm.

At its peak Fairthorpe cars employed 50 people manufacturing several hundred cars a year. Three men could make a body in one day and only two men were needed to produce the excellent chassis in the same time. They went into the kit-car business and Don Bennett's son Torix took part in running what became a highly efficient enterprise — until new legislation came along. Type Approval was demanded and the cost of obtaining such approval was beyond the resources of a small firm like Fairthorpe. So what could have grown into a job-providing, export-earning concern is now reduced to making spares for the many Fairthorpe cars still in use all over the world.

Don Bennett had a hankering to manufacture light aircraft. He built a pre-war ultralight, the Dart Kitten before his attention was captivated by a delightful French design called the Emerauld. It had eliptical wings like a little Spitfire and a comfortable cabin with side-by-side seating for two. The

Emerauld performed well on its 100 hp engine and Don Bennett set up a small works at Denham where he built a slightly modified version called the Fairtravel Linnet. Wings, tail units, fuselage etc were taken by road to Blackbushe airfield near Camberley where assembly and flight testing was enacted. In those days £2450 would buy a new Linnet complete with a good flight panel but after only seven aircraft had been completed the government of the day subsidised the Beagle aircraft company, at the time engaged in the production of a light twin and the Pup single-engined trainer. Bennett was unable to compete with this state-sponsored concern and, once again, private enterprise run at no cost to the tax-payer was winged in its fledgeling days. Donald Bennett seems to have suffered more than his fair share of official discouragement in the course of trying to create new industries on a walk-before-you-run basis. The state had a totally different approach to new industries in those days. It believed in pouring in money by the million, consequently a money-no-object atmosphere prevailed from the word 'go', grand offices, expensive hired help and jobs-for-the-boys were all part of a national sickness which was partly the result of refusing to face the facts. The Bennett way was to start small, gain product acceptance and, if successful, expand. There was nothing new in this concept; it was a long-established principle of sound business. Left to get on with the job in peace Bennett the car-maker and Bennett the 'plane-maker would have succeeded to the benefit of all concerned. But the men from the ministry intervened, the state poured in the millions — and the nation lost.

Before the war there were in Britain fifteen or more separate companies making some of the finest light aircraft in the world. This is no chauvinistic opinion from an over-patriotic Englishman; when in 1936 the great Charles Lindbergh wanted a high-speed, long-range light aircraft for his own personal use it was to Phillips & Powis Aircraft Ltd of Reading (later Miles Aircraft) that he turned.

After the war a combination of impoverished national finance, unrealistic thinking and over-regulation by the authorities coupled with the burden of excessive charges for registration, airworthiness requirements and landing fees combined to see the gradual demise of the British light aircraft industry. This was accompanied by the closing of airfields on a scale that was in direct contrast to other countries where the value of light aviation was better appreciated. In France, for example, there is hardly a small country town that does not have its own airfield. It may be no more than a grass strip but the facility is there for the local flying school and visiting company aircraft which bring business and prosperity to the area. By contrast the important town of Portsmouth in the south of England (population more than 220,000) closed its airfield many years ago. The decline of British light aviation and the systematic closing of local airfields, often by local councils who, at best acted through lack of knowledge or, at worst, sheer envy because flying was wrongly believed to be only for the wealthy, was a matter of grave concern to Don Bennett. So it was at Blackbushe, a large airfield situated five miles north west of Farnborough, famous home of the international air show held every two years. He knew the airfield well. Among other operators Fairflight had used it as a base but now Fairflight was gone, other firms had also left and local councils were casting their greedy eyes on the land with ambitions of carving up the runways and taking steps calculated to bring some of their members financial advantage. Loss of Blackbushe with its fine runways, good weather record and ideal situation would have been a serious blow to aviation and, in the long term, the British nation. All this was a closed book to those of an anti-aviation mind and plans were made to dismantle the airfield, turn it into common land and engage in various projects that would have done little for the surrounding countryside. But they reckoned without the Master Airman.

Chapter 13
The Blackbushe Affair

With Fairflight ceasing operations the company name was adopted, with Don Bennett's agreement, by a Biggin Hill based concern. The premises at Blackbushe Airport were vacated. Then Silver City, another independent operator, left the airport and others followed.

Ownership of the airfield was complex to define. Parts of the runways belonged to a parish council which did not care for airfields or aeroplanes. The Air Ministry owned a little of the airfield but much of the land belonged to Sir Richard Calthorpe. It eventually transpired that owners of land adjacent to the airfield were intent on its closure so that their own investment could be developed. There is, of course, nothing wrong in wishing to profit from one's investment but when position on a local council is used to further personal ambitions of a financial nature this degrades both the individual and local government.

A number of people approached Don Bennett and asked what could be done to save the airfield. It had developed during the war and now the emergency was over all manner of land titles needed looking into before any steps were taken to purchase the airfield. For example there was the matter of 'rights of common'. Bennett went to the Air Ministry who assured him that having looked closely into that facet of the law for several years they were convinced that no rights of common were applicable to the airfield although there may well be such public rights in the surrounding area. Bennett visited Winchester County Library and obtained two copies of a covenant drawn up in 1567, one in Latin, the other written in old English. These gave rights of covenant on 'waste lands of the manor' whereby the public was free to take 'moss, fern and rough timber'. There were no grazing rights. Bennett searched ancient church records but he was unable to find any evidence to support rights of common on the land occupied by Blackbushe Airport. An approach was made to the Aviation Minister of the day (Peter Thornycroft) who made clear his support for the airfield provided it did not draw away air traffic from Gatwick, an airport nearer London then being developed at considerable cost by the state. Notwithstanding these assurances the mood of the parish council and indeed Hampshire County Council was well known to Bennett. It was a foregone conclusion that he could expect every possible opposition if he tried to save the airfield and operate it. So why did he buy it?

"Just sheer desperation. Everyone was trying to destroy everything in aviation. They wanted to close Blackbushe, turn it back to the wilds when it was an excellent airport with the best weather record anywhere near London."

Bennett had served on a committee chaired by Sir Henry Self in 1946 and it had envisaged seven airports for the London area. Blackbushe, with its excellent runways and good weather should certainly be one of these. Yet he would drive along the main road and note with dismay the destruction of airport buildings.

In 1961 the Air Ministry sold its interests in Blackbushe to Don Bennett and so did the Calthorpe family. Now he owned 75 per cent of the runways and the Minister had given his blessings for general aviation to prosper at the airfield. Naturally Blackbushe would have to be licensed by the civil aviation authorities and a good starting point would be to form a flying club. Bennett called a meeting that July at the Hawley Hotel, Blackwater. There a number of people agreed to form the Blackbushe Aero Club. At first the school was run on a voluntary basis but eventually paid staff took over. Lord Trefgarne ran the club for some time until his political activities became too pressing.

Why had Blackbushe come to the brink of extinction only to be rescued at the eleventh hour by Don Bennett? Responsibility must clearly rest with the Minister of Transport and Civil Aviation of 1959, Harold Watkinson who, if he achieved little else for his country's aviation, certainly had a good track record for closing down airfields. Under his leadership the Ministry regarded Blackbushe as a threat to Gatwick and set about destroying its facilities. 400 or so drains were filled with concrete, buildings and hangars were demolished, runways damaged, water supplies, electric services and telephone lines were ripped out along with new airfield lighting, only recently installed at the then considerable cost of £60,000. By the time the authorities had finished their vandalism the airfield looked like a disaster area and anyone seeing it could have been excused for saying "No aircraft will ever fly from here again." Lesser characters would have given up but Donald Clifford Tyndall Bennett was not the kind of man to be daunted by the task or intimated by local councils.

From its first, faltering days, the reprieved Blackbushe Airport was an object of constant attack from the local councils. Opposition was being orchestrated often by those with vested interests, and various newspapers, all of them sympathetically disposed towards the plan to save the airfield, stand on record as a monument to local government at its worst. Don Bennett appeared at meetings and reminded the anti-aviation brigade that many people previously employed by the various firms who until recently had based themselves at Blackbushe were local residents. They had bought houses adjacent to the airfield. Now that Fairflight, Silver City and other companies had departed these same people would naturally welcome the re-activation of this important airfield. Then there was the growing interest in corporate aviation — aircraft owned by large concerns who used them to meet their customers in Europe or even further afield. Blackbushe was of great value to them. He also reminded the various councils that because of anti-aviation attitudes such as theirs Britain had lost its light aircraft industry to America and France. It was all to no avail — blind eyes and deaf ears.

Typical of the opposition being engineered at the time was a letter from a retired senior Naval officer published in the local press which said "Would it not be better to treat the application [to operate Blackbushe as an airfield] as from a private individual status, rather than rely upon continual emphasis of the Air Vice-Marshal's war record — " while other ill-informed protest asked "Are we to surrender the rural peace of the majority for a student pilot circling round and round the airfield in attempts to remain airborne?" That worthy clearly wanted aviation to go away. Because if one cannot operate a flying school in open country, well away from highly built-up areas, where can such flying take place? The like minded, who would have the world believe that low powered light aircraft are noisy often regard as socially acceptable motor mowers, high-fi, sports cars, fast motorcycles and so forth, all of them making more noise than the average light 'plane.

Hampshire County Council rejected by eleven votes to three Don Bennett's application to fly from his own airfield. All manner of irrelevant reasons were given including the claim that flying activities would 'interfere with the safety and free flow of traffic on the nearby trunk road', a statement hardly likely to support the campaign of obstruction being waged by Hampshire County Council. Because here was a clear admission that light and general aviation was of great interest to the general public. Possibly the worthy councillors felt they had a mission to tell the nation what it should or should not like, and to make their point by denying those who wished to fly the necessary facilities.

Pettiness reached new heights when Yately councillors lodged a complaint with the War Minister because some off-duty Guards officers had the temerity to land at Blackbushe in a light 'plane belonging to their aero club. Also the Chairman of a local council was reported to have threatened that he would himself take a sledge hammer and break down a sign pointing to Blackbushe Airport. By now councillors of various local authorities were behaving like spoiled children, castigating everyone from Don Bennett, the editor of the *Camberley News,* a local car club and, of course, all people who fly. Much of the hostility found its roots in the cult of envy — 'I can't fly so why should you.' One council member was foolish enough to walk on to the runway in an attempt to get the registration of a flying aircraft. He later complained at a council meeting that he had to duck 'because the landing aircraft was so low.' The worthy councillor was obviously unaware that before an aircraft can land it is a weakness of the vehicle that it must get itself near to the ground.

In the main the various local newspapers being circulated in the surrounding areas supported Bennett in his fight to save Blackbushe from being destroyed by authorities that should have known better. Reading these newspapers it seems clear that Hampshire County Council had made up its mind to schedule the airport as a public place although there were already 8700 acres of such land in the area. Such was the council's determination to destroy the airport that they claimed 300 acres of Bennett's land for the purpose. The absurdity of their case was not lost on the Aviation Minister and matters came to a head when at a public hearing called in May 1962 Dr. Hill, Minister of Housing and Local Government, overruled Hampshire County Council and granted permission for the re-opening of Blackbushe Airport while the Minister of Aviation welcomed Don Bennett's enterprise. On 11 September that year NOTAM 617 was issued by the Ministry of Aviation announcing that 'Blackbushe aerodrome is now licensed and available to civil aircraft.

They celebrated the opening of the airport with a two hour air display. One member of the local public wrote to the *Aldershot News* and claimed that the main noise came from heavy traffic on the nearby trunk road, not the aircraft. However, the battle was not yet over. Astonishing as it may seem after two ministries had given their approval for Blackbushe to operate as an airport nearby Yately Council pressed a claim that Don Bennett's land was not freehold and that the public had right of access. Rumours were generated and spread, by whom it was never proved, to the effect that the airfield would soon be opened up to the big jets. Fortunately for aviation its loudest critics rarely know very much about the subject and this rumour had been concocted in total ignorance of the fact that the big jets required runways twice the size of those at Blackbushe. One or two letters appeared in the local press claiming that the 150 seat VC10 four-jet airliner (then in service with BOAC, British United Airlines and others) could operate from Bennett's private Heathrow. So they could. But no-one explained why they should wish to visit Blackbushe, which had no passenger handling facilities, when bigger and far better equipped airports were located nearer London.

To dispel unfounded fears and stop rumours Don Bennett tried to address various councils but tricks of procedure were employed to deny him a fair hearing. The situation was complicated by the fact that part of the main runway was owned by Yately Council and, in an attempt to inconvenience pilots, its officials had thought fit to order that a trench be cut where their bit ended and Bennett's began. They owned land adjacent to the airfield and following a village meeting, where those present were claimed to have voted against Blackbushe enjoying access, Don Bennett was approached by a number of people who thought they had voted in his favour only to find that the form produced at the meeting had misled them. As a result of these representations Don Bennett issued a High Court writ against Lt. Commander Michael Chappell, the Yately Parish Council Chairman and its twelve members. He was not successful.

Meanwhile Blackbushe continued operating on the land owned by Don Bennett. At the end of its first year of operation the Blackbushe Aero Club had 200 members, it could look back with pride and some satisfaction that its founder had saved the airfield from destruction, having fought off the combined assault of three or four councils. A number of non-flying firms rented accommodation on the airfield and, to his credit, Don Bennett even allowed other flying schools to set up shop in competition with his own. Notwithstanding all this activity life in the surrounding villages went on as usual but, of course, the original anti-flying hysteria had little to do with noise. It was motivated by deeper psychological forces, some political (affronted officialdom) others inspired by financial interests while envy of those who flew added yet another ingredient to the senseless bickering. Some villains spread roofing tacks and broken glass on the main runway, an act that could have caused a fatal accident and while it is not suggested that this was the work of local councillor their own behaviour was almost as irresponsible and likely to encourage such acts. According to the *Reading Mercury* of 17 September, 1966 Hampshire County Council erected a gipsy housing estate within 150 feet of, and in direct line with, one of the runways. They even threatened to plant a row of trees across the ends of the other runways. Long after the airport was well and truly established, and clearly there to stay, this same council tried to demand the removal of the flying club building on the grounds that it had been built on 'common land', something that had already been disproved. In the case that followed Judge Claude Duveen QC found for Don Bennett at Aldershot County Court. He accused the council of using the case to discourage Bennett from erecting necessary buildings at Blackbushe Airport which was " — providing a service to the country."

County Council hostility continued. Eight planning applications at the airport were turned down and in each case Don Bennett was put to the expensive and time wasting inconvenience of having to appeal. The Ministry of Housing and Local Government upheld his appeals on every occasion but that is hardly surprising. The council had no real reason for being obstructive other than an obsessional desire to thwart Don Bennett. In place of a case based on substance, the faceless Town Hall wonders had no more than excuses and obtuse technical reasons to justify their hostility towards the airport. At one public enquiry held under the chairmanship of a Ministry of Housing Inspector Don Bennett complained of the " — senseless vendetta" that had been conducted against him over a period of five years by Hampshire County Council. He asked why the officials concerned failed to understand that aircraft need hangars. And why was it considered unreasonable of him to want a restaurant on the airport. No doubt they were unaware that most little grass airfields in France offer food to visitors, often on a scale that stands comparison with a high class city restaurant. They had even refused him permission to erect a fence!

As if having to contend with vindictive, under-employed Town Hall officials was not enough, a number of retired senior army officers demanded a right of way across the airfield, totally disregarding the obvious risk to aircraft and people alike. In an effort to bring down the temperature in the area Bennett put forward a plan that the eleven local authorities with peripheral or more intimate interest in the airport should jointly take over Blackbushe and develop it. This was a generous offer; he had government support for running the airfield, every planning appeal had been found in his favour and the councils might have been expected to react in a civilised manner to the hand of friendship now being extended. Quite the reverse; not only was there no support for the plan, every possible obstruction was devised to try and prevent Don Bennett from running an efficient airfield, fortunately with little success. Wing Commander Bill Freeman came from Staverton Airport to manage Blackbushe and bear the brunt of the Local Authority attacks.

One of Don Bennett's less successful tenants was a gentleman with ideas of running aeroplanes and helicopters for security purposes. They would be linked by radio to police cars and the enterprise started on a lavish scale with thirty staff. At the end of two weeks there was no money to pay the wages.

Secretary at the Blackbushe Aero Club and general tower of strength at the time was Mrs Dorothy Grey. She remembers the day when on his way back from the Continent Don Bennett had run into reducing visibility while flying his de Havilland Dove. Prudence dictated that he should clear customs at Lympne Airport near Folkestone before pressing on into the unknown. The telephone rang in Bill Freeman's office. "Go and look at the western side of the airfield" said Bennett. Sometimes that end of Blackbushe enjoyed better weather than the eastern part of the airfield. This was one of those occasions so he said "Right, I'm coming in." He positioned over nearby Farnborough, caught a glimpse of an aircraft on the ground, then let down into the mist on his watch and made an immaculate landing on Blackbushe. It was a reminder of his professionalism in the days when flying brought in the bread and butter. On another occasion he flew back from Cannes in his Linnet, G-ASZR. Stuart Marshall was an assistant air traffic controller in the tower at the time and he remembers advising Bennett that the cloud base over Blackbushe was only 200 feet and it was pouring with rain. It was one of those days when, to use an aviation phrase, even the birds were walking. Bennett had no radio other than a simple transmitter-receiver but he broke cloud over the centre of the airfield and made a perfect landing. Such a performance by an average pilot would have been foolhardy; to Don Bennett it was just a routine piece of flying.

Less professional, and an uncomfortable re-enactment of the time when he found himself flying a Tudor in bad weather at night with the elevator locks in place, was an incident which again involved one of his own Linnets. Chief Flying Instructor at the Blackbushe Aero Club in those days was John Varley, AFC, a retired BOAC Senior Captain with more than 30,000 flying hours in many types of aircraft ranging from light two-seat trainers to Boeing 707 passenger jets. Like most pilots with a long and successful career he kept his neck intact by exercising the kind of self discipline that is an essential part of good airmanship. Towards the end of his training the student pilot has to face the General Flying Test and John was in the process of completing one of these with a member of the club. "Show me how you would park the aircraft in the open for any length of time" requested the veteran pilot. This was a good student and he knew what was required of him. The controls were tied back to stop them being blown about. Chocks were placed against the wheels and the pitot cover, a glove-like device which fits over the pressure/static tube that samples air for the altimeter, vertical speed indicator and airspeed indicator, was duly tied in place to prevent dust or other debris from entering the works and prejudicing instrument indications. Yes indeed, this student pilot had done his homework and John Varley was well pleased.

A few moments later Don Bennett arrived, announced that he was going to fly the aircraft locally. Nothing more was heard until he returned and admitted rather sheepishly that he had taken off only to discover that his airspeed indicator was not working — he had not done a proper pre-flight check so he had taken off with the pitot cover on, its long, red warning pennant streaming in the the airflow. The retired Air Vice-Marshal got little sympathy from John Varley who looked him in the eye and mentioned the words 'pre flight checks'. Nothing more was said.

Dorothy Grey found Don Bennett to be a considerate boss, very kind to the women who worked for him at the airfield, (Pat Goddard, Mary Budd and Audrey Anderson) but he was sometimes inclined towards the intolerant with male members of the staff. However he would stand by them in times of trouble. There was a petty and trivial storm in a tea cup brewed up by one of the local councils. Holland Birkett, chairman of the

Blackbushe Aero Club, had been killed along with his wife while flying in France. Don Bennett thought it would be a nice gesture to name a lane leading to the airport after their deceased friends. Along came the heavy hand of local government. "You can't do this," they said in outrage, "only the council can name streets." So they pulled down the sign which said *Birkett Lane* and in place put up *Little Vigo*. Some person unknown, objecting to this high-handed behaviour decided to pull up the sign and throw it into some nearby bushes. A local publican told the police he had seen John Varley commit this heinous crime. Now nothing more representative of law and order exists than the retired airline captain and the idea of this dignified figure, with his trim, grey beard, ripping up street names to pass the time of day is laughable. Nevertheless the police accepted the publican's word and prosecuted John Varley who was found guilty. Bennett engaged a barrister, John lodged an appeal and he was subsequently cleared of all charges.

Much has been said in this chapter about the constant obstruction and harrassment suffered by Don Bennett at the hand of local government. It is, of course, right and proper that folk who have elected to enjoy the peace and tranquility of country life should have their interests protected. But there are limits to everything; others have a right to live too and light aircraft make no more noise than the average petrol mower, probably less than a two stroke. The traumas of Blackbushe Airport that were perpetrated by the various authorities involved in the long, drawn-out disputes were an example of local government at its most perverse. Those concerned came out of the long running battle with egg on their faces. Don Bennett, on the other hand, had championed a worthwhile cause, taken on all comers and emerged with the future of Blackbushe assured. However the cost of having to appeal against the unreasonable behaviour of the local authorities whenever a planning application was refused on nebulous grounds was more than he could reasonably be expected to bear. It could even be argued that he had been under no obligation to seek planning permission for some of the developments because Blackbushe had long been an established airfield. As long ago as 1894 regular Balloon Meetings had been held on the site and during the 1914-18 war it had acted as an important satellite airfield to nearby Farnborough, then home of the Royal Aircraft Factory. Furthermore in 1940 a runway was put down and the area became known as RAF Station Hartford Bridge Flats. However appeals against misguided local authorities are expensive and eventually Don Bennett sold the airfield to Mr D. Arnold who some years later disposed of it to the present owners who are intent on safeguarding the future of this valuable general aviation airport.

Not long after the war two very large civil aircraft were built. There was the massive Brabazon landplane designed and constructed by the Bristol Aeroplane Company and an even heavier flying boat called the Princess which was the work of Saunders Roe. Both projects were overtaken by the march of progress and for some years the three magnificent Princess boats were cocooned, moored in wrappings to await a decision on their future. At one time the Winder Aircraft Corporation of Florida, USA, had ideas of using them as flying test beds for atomic powered aero engines but these plans came to nought. Don Bennett made a bid for two of these enormous flying boats which were many times larger than the Short Empire boats he had flown with Imperial Airways before the war but nothing came of these plans either.

So for Don Bennett the Blackbushe saga came to an end when he sold the airport, having achieved most of what he set out to do. For some time he maintained an office on the airfield and there he engaged himself in a number of political activities which, in the main, have proved less successful and have brought him less satisfaction than many of his other persuits.

Chapter 14
Bennett, the man

When asked, somewhat accusingly, why he had almost invariably supported AVM Cochran whenever that officer had a difference of opinion with Bennett, Marshal of the Royal Air Force Sir Arthur Harris felt moved to admit that, nine times out of ten, Bennett proved to be right. Consider the implications of that statement by a great man and imagine what kind of paradise on earth would be the lot of the human species if nine times out of ten doctors and politicians were right. This engaging hypothesis was put to Don Bennett and then the question was asked — if you were right on nine occasions out of ten when, in your view, did you make a mistake that was a cause of regret. He thought for a moment and said —

'I think I was wrong to go into party politics at all. I was bounced into it on the spur of the moment, under pressure, and I wish I hadn't. Because you are immediately labelled. Whatever you feel inside yourself other people don't know that. And they think "he is that awful party that unseated our so-and-so, split the vote or did something or other he shouldn't have done" '.

Then he added —

'I wish we had had two more children, but the war came along.'

Although Bennett regards the brief encounter with party politics as an error of judgement many of his admirers regret his involvement with politics in any form at all, particularly the various pressure groups, some of them laudable but others which cannot have advanced his own cause. A stranger meeting Bennett would regard him as a type-cast Englishman, but Don Bennett is, in many respects, very much an Australian. And while there is much common ground between the two species Australians are nevertheless as different to Englishmen as Englishmen are to Americans. Each nationality has its strengths and weaknesses.

The complacency of the British certainly exists although it is often more apparent than real. It has sometimes proved to be a powerful secret weapon; in two world wars the Germans greatly underestimated the British. Likewise this apparent complacency is a source of both bewilderment and irritation among Australians and Americans who share a mutual get-up-and-go attitude to life and a mistrust of what they regard to be pompous behaviour. On the other hand a characteristic of many Australians is a taste for strong opinions and, in this respect, Don Bennett is your true, no-nonsense citizen from down under.

Many of his strongly held beliefs have been proved correct, often in the face of united, so-called expert opinions to the contrary. One such opinion is a near-obsessional dislike of the European Common Market which has, on several occasions, found him in bed with strange company. However, many of his long-standing friends will tell you that Don Bennett would sup with the Devil himself if he thought that would extract Britain from the EEC. Why does he so dislike that organisation? In his own words:-

'I was a founder member of the European Movement. Sir Walter Layton and I were close friends in 1944 and we evolved our ideas about a European Community. Now that is not anti-Europe; that is pro-Europe. We looked at it from the point of view of a voluntary association of the European nations — voluntarily co-ordinating and collectively working out schemes of co-operation.

After the war, when incidentally I was still chairman of the United Nations Association, I was a member of the Hague conference which was set up to get Europe co-operating. The British delegation was headed by a chap called Churchill and I was one of the junior members.

I was pro-Europe. The choice before that assembly was our plan — the European Free Trade Area, as it became, or EEC which was the Schumann plan (Schumann being a German-born Frenchman) adequately supported by Spaak, the Belgian Prime Minister. They wanted to go the whole hog of compulsion; we wanted to stay free. So we separated. EFTA was formed straight away. It was a complete free trade area within its membership and without any barriers outside.

EEC has the common tariff barrier. Nothing may come in, or if it does it is taxed, not by us — we don't get the money. It is taxed by Brussels. And incidentally it is a rather interesting thing that even to this day there is no declaration as to how much money goes to Brussels direct. The only thing that is ever published is what we pay them extra to the automatic levies and VAT.

All I am saying is we can co-operate and we should co-operate. But it should be on a free basis and it should not be at the expense of our friends. These people [a reference to some Europeans] are either our enemies or supporters of our enemies in fairly well established positions. To say that we should support them, and trade only with them — not take New Zealand butter or Australian beef — is stinking in my view and absolutely disgusting. And I don't mind who knows it. To say that we should destroy our sovereignty is to say we are traitors. And my version of a traitor is one who would destroy the independence of his own people."

No doubt there are many who share Don Bennett's very strong views on Britain's role in the EEC but in the course of expressing his opinions at various public meetings the National Front on one or perhaps more occasions managed to present itself in a way that looked as though Don Bennett was addressing their organisation as a sympathiser if not himself a member. *The Guardian* of 8 September 1972 reported on a meeting being held by porters at the Smithfield market. They were in protest at the arrival of Ugandan Asians and although only 50 or so actually marched through London to Smith Square the total number was inflated to some 400 people by the arrival of Hells' Angels and the National Front. The meeting was addressed by Don Bennett. A year earlier in the 14 November, 1971 edition of the same national newspaper was a report that —

'Air Vice-Marshal Donald Bennett, 61, the British war hero who led Bomber Command's famous Pathfinder force against Nazi Germany, is to take part in a National Front ceremony at the Cenotaph today.'

Naturally this contradiction — an apparent sympathy for British Fascists from the man who so effectively fought their German inspirers, was the subject of an interview. In it he expressed his wish to honour the dead of Rhodesia, South Africa and Northern Ireland. The previous year flags of Rhodesia and South Africa had been banned. Looking back on these occasions Don Bennett is adamant that it was not he who joined forces with the National Front, quite the reverse; they attached themselves to him —

'That is the National Front technique. They find out there is a rally somewhere, or even a sporting event, and they go along and tag on.'

He is aware that in some quarters there are those who accuse him of holding extreme, right wing views, and on one occasion he issued a writ against the Young Socialists for claiming in print that he was a member of a Fascist organisation, however those who have known him well for many years describe him differently. They see Don Bennett as a liberal with a small 'l', against the party system and totally dedicated to Britain's extraction from the EEC. He will tell you, rather resignedly — 'I am also supposed to be a radical left-winger' and in the same breath 'I am an insatiable reformer. I see things that are wrong and I tend to say so, whereas most other people are much more diplomatic. I'm not. Things like the party system of government; you wouldn't run a cricket club or a tennis club on a basis of half the people being in opposition, trying to stop you, and the other half trying to run it. You negotiate, you talk, you discuss things. You decide on merit on every subject. Not so the government of this country. Parliament goes along — slanging matches, throwing things at each other and generally being destructive as opposed to constructive — I think it's wrong.'

In furtherance of these beliefs he set up the Political Freedom Movement of which he is Chairman. It advocates banishment of the Party Whip system and free voting by Members of Parliament on every issue. These views are expanded in a little booklet written by Don Bennett entitled *Let us Try Democracy*. However, uppermost in his mind are the activities of the British Anti-Common Market Campaign, an all-party pressure group of which he is one of the national vice-chairmen. In essence he would like to see Britain free to trade more strongly within what he likes to call the Crown Commonwealth. And to those who, fearing the consequences of leaving the EEC, ask the question 'What would we then do?' he answers firmly 'We would do precisely what we want to do.'

His critics, and indeed some of his friends, have been known to say that he is inclined to be politically naive, and that he dissipates his talents by involving himself in pressure groups, some of which represent lost causes. In discussing some of his post-war political activities with him one has the impression that many of his liaisons, although well motivated, were entered into without a full realisation that hidden within often laudable aims were others of a less admirable nature. This has led some bodies, particularly those closely involved with minority persecution, to accuse him of being a racist. Nevertheless, his firm denial of this charge is supported by those who have known him well over a long period. How does he feel about coloured immigration into Britain?

'Well, we have three million unemployed. Why should we open the doors to anybody? To put it bluntly, Macmillan thought he was going to get some cheap labour.'

His recognition of, and regret for the plight of unemployed blacks is also tinged with anger at the way some people think it fashionable to be ashamed of being white, but some of the misconceptions about Don Bennett may well be of his own making. Ly Bennett had, on occasions, warned her husband that many of those present at meetings may not have been able to follow his line of argument, or even fully understand the perfectly valid points he was trying to make. According to Ly Bennett —

'Trouble is he does not always explain himself clearly because he assumes they understand. He has a brilliant brain but he is so lacking in conceit he expects the most ordinary people to follow him. He never talks down to people.'

Not talking down to people may, on occasions, have caused him to be misunderstood at political meetings but this same remarkable characteristic of being able to communicate with the office boy as though the lad were managing director has, in peace and war extracted from all manner of folk talents and hidden abilities they never thought could exist within themselves. When Don Bennett lost his appointment as chief of British South American Airways and set up Airflight much of the day-to-day running was left to Ly. She found herself taking bookings, working out complex charter quotations — even interviewing pilots applying for jobs. It was all new ground to her but husband Don's complete trust and total acceptance that she could do the job made her tackle daily problems in a way that, in retrospect, is a source of considerable surprise at her own achievements.

Don Bennett has been described, often by those who have never met him, as 'enigmatic', 'austere,' 'lacking in humour' and so forth. It should be remembered that as a young man barely 33 years of age he had under his command in 8 Group some 22,000 men and women. The great majority never had an opportunity of meeting him; it was not possible for a hard-pressed group commander to shake hands with all his airmen and airwomen in times of war. Consequently the legend of Bennett, the young genius of aviation, grew, like most legends, with all manner of old wives tales surrounding truth. He was a 'puritan' because he didn't drink yet the background to that is simple. In the days when Don Bennett was a lad in Queensland Australia you were either a totally committed drunk or you never touched the stuff. There were no half measures, so Don chose the sober life and the habit stuck. At an early age he recognised the futility of smoking but these two 'unfashionable' habits, non-smoking and non-drinking, have sometimes made him an object of suspicion among simple-minded folk.

One of Bennett's favourite saying is — 'The Perfect is the enemy of the Very Good' however, dedication to professionalism was another characteristic that helped build up a distorted image of the man. There was the case of a Flight Sergeant Wireless Operator. He had taken part in a number of operations and his squadron commander thought fit to put him up for a commission. So he was duly summoned to appear before his AOC at 8 Group Headquarters. "And how many words a minute can you read in morse?" asked Don Bennett. "Twenty-four sir" replied the Flight Sergeant whereupon his AOC opened a drawer and took out a small, battery operated morse buzzer of the type used for practice at the Wireless Operator training schools in those days. He told the Flight Sergeant to write down the message he was about to send. Don Bennett started tapping away and after a few moments an embarrassed young man had to say "Sorry sir — I was unable to get it all down." Bennett tried again, this time at a rather slower rate, but once more the Flight Sergeant was several words behind. At that stage Don Bennett said "Go away Flight Sergeant, learn your profession, then come and see me again." Naturally, versions of this interview flashed around that Flight Sergeant's squadron and beyond. The sensible recognised the rightness of Don Bennett's action. After all, Britain was fighting a war against an enemy, large in numbers, well equipped, often highly trained and the RAF was hardly likely to beat such an enemy on an amateur basis. But professionalism is often an object of suspicion, consequently one researches a book such as this to find that although there were very few people who did not admire Don Bennett only those who dealt with him directly really liked him. And in the main, those who got to know him would almost without exception have done anything for Don Bennett. 'Bomber' Harris once said:-

'He tended to be shy; only those who knew him well really understood Bennett and such friendships have proved lasting.'

If he has a serious fault it is his inability to recognise that others are rarely able to match his own outstanding pilot skills or attain the same levels of diverse knowledge. A typical example of this was recounted by the late Squadron Leader Laurie Kelly, at one time a flying instructor at the prestigious Empire Central Flying School which operated at RAF Hullavington during the war. Later he instructed at the Pathfinder Mosquito conversion school where pilots, often experienced, came for their first introduction to the 'Wooden Wonder'. One day the weather was terrible — low cloud, poor visibility and everything dripping wet. It was the kind of day when, to use the fashionable language of 1939-1945, 'even the birds were walking.'

The crew room was full of students and instructors when Bennett walked in unannounced. Everyone sprang to their feet as he demanded "Why aren't you chaps flying?" One of the braver instructors muttered something about the weather and without a word, Bennett walked out of the room then across the apron to a line of Mosquitos dripping with moisture. He climbed into one of them, started up, taxied out and took off to disappear almost immediately in low cloud. A few moments later he appeared like a shadow emerging from the gloom to make a perfect landing and taxi to the parking lot. Faces at the crew room windows disappeared as he walked across the apron, entered the room and announced "There's nothing wrong with the weather — get airborne."

Confronted by this story in recent times he countered with the words "Yes but I never asked anyone to do anything I would not do myself." That is all very well but few could match his capabilities and then there was the matter of experience. A minimum of 700 hours flying was required before a pilot would be considered for conversion to Mosquitos and in those days 1000-hour pilots were regarded as a race apart. In contrast, Don Bennett had some 9000 hours or more in his log book, much of it instrument flying, and what was easy for him assumed mammoth proportions to most other wartime pilots.

He would argue that such behaviour on his part brought out the best in people and events may well have proved him right. Certainly he had an uncanny nose for avoiding psychological problems with his aircrews. During the war lurid posters were printed on all manner of subjects and one of these depicted a Mosquito, an undercarriage leg collapsed, the wings at a drunken angle, a propeller bent and flames bursting from the engine behind it. In bold letters underneath were the words —

DON'T LET A SWING DEVELOP

Don Bennett saw these posters, recognised their intimidating nature and, according to Laurie Kelly, said "Get them all down."

The offending posters disappeared from the walls of Pathfinder Force; Mosquito take-off and landing accidents improved almost immediately.

However strongly he may feel about any issue, and he can be deeply upset by what he regards as injustice, he nevertheless has a strong sense of loyalty that transcends personal feelings. His wartime attitude towards Sir Arthur Harris is a prime example of this:-

'My relationship with Bert [Harris] is that we are friends and I have always been loyal to him. I think we have a lot of mutual respect. But it doesn't alter the fact that he did some things to me that were really shocking' [a reference to the removal of 617 Squadron which Bennett regarded as a slight on the good name of Pathfinder Force.]

There can be no doubt that the late Sir Arthur Harris held Don Bennett in the highest esteem. This came across in conversation and in his book, *Bomber Offensive*, the great war leader said —

'He was, and still is, the most efficient airman I have ever met.'

However, later in the book there is a reference to a side of Don Bennett in his younger days that unquestionably made him a number of enemies:-

'His courage, both moral and physical, is outstanding, and as a technician he is unrivalled. He will forgive me if I say that his consciousness of his own intellectual powers sometimes made him impatient with slower or differently constituted minds, so that some people found him difficult to work with. He could not suffer fools gladly, and by his own high standards there were many fools.'

It is an irony of human relations that the many of us who are endowed with average or perhaps below average abilities tend to resent the few who are gifted. One often hears of the intolerance of clever people but what of the other side of the penny — the refusal of people unable to see or understand to accept the word of those with a talent for seeing the situation and its remedy in utter clarity. It may well be that the brilliant young Bennett was unable to disguise his irritation with stupidity from above (he was rarely impatient with his subordinates — only the bosses got stick from Bennett). But there was a war on, Britain's position was desperate and senior officers with a Sopwith Camel mentality were standing in his way, frustrating the sound advice he was offering the C-in-C Bomber Command.

The war years so occupied his every working hour that there was little time to spend with the children and at the end of the conflict his daughter Noreen, then only a child, had no idea of the important role taken by her father. However, she was later to marry an RAF Officer, now Air Commodore Geoffrey Cooper (retired), Air Correspondent of *The Daily Telegraph*.

What was the true value of Don Bennett's contribution to the war effort? To comprehend this it is first necessary to understand the magnitude of Bomber Command's achievements. Under Arthur Harris, Bomber command forced the Germans to withdraw great quantities of military equipment and manpower for the defence of the Fatherland. More than two million service personnel were engaged on anti-aircraft work, mine sweeping and so forth. All this equipment had to be moved from Occupied Europe and the Russian fronts. Eventually 75 per cent of Germany's fighter and anti-aircraft capabilities were tied down by Bomber Command. According to Albert Speer, Hitler's Reichmarshal of Industry, between one million and one-and-a-half million people were engaged in air raid precautions and salvage operations. A total of almost a million tons of bombs were dropped by Bomber Command during the 68 months of war. They destroyed a high proportion of Germany's vital industry. During 1944 no complete gun left the Krupps works in Essen. At Bochum war production was down to 14 per cent, coal output was halved and steel deliveries declined to 15 per cent of normal. In Dortmund steel and engineering production declined to only 40 per cent and by March 1945 the town was at a standstill. Dusseldorf suffered a 50 per cent loss of electric power and Hamburg sustained the destruction of 130,000 tons of goods, oil production was reduced to only 25 per cent, 180,000 tons of shipping were sunk and 130 U-boats under construction were denied the German Navy. The list is endless. All this had a devastating effect on the Nazi war machine and when the Allies re-entered Europe Germany's superb army had lost the will or the means to stem the advancing tide. And when Von Rundstedt made his brilliant counter attack, which posed a threat of crisis proportions to the Allied ground forces, the situation was made even more traumatic by the possible withdrawal of air support because fog covered the area. Indeed, it grounded the German and American air forces; the RAF kept flying and, with the aid of OBOE, bombed the German troop concentrations into a state of shocked inactivity.

By the end of the war German oil production was practically destroyed and more of her naval vessels had been sunk from the air than as a result of action by the Royal Navy. It is not the purpose of this book to deprecate the fine contribution of the United States Air Force, far from it. They were heavily committed in the Pacific. But in so far as Europe is concerned its activities were on a very much smaller scale than RAF Bomber Command. Even the so called Mosquito 'nuisance' raids on Berlin were far more devastating than the worst raids on London.

After the war left wing opinion could often be heard deploring the success of Bomber Command and even now there are people who are convinced that Britain was wrong to have bombed Germany. When it is suggested that, without the efforts of Bomber Command the rescue of Western Europe may have been impossible and Britain would ultimately have become another slave state under the Nazi heel, no coherent answers are forthcoming.

A prime example of this thinking, which at its most charitable can only be described as lacking in realism, was an editorial printed in a leading London newspaper during 1985 under the heading "One Night in Dresden". The burden of this sanctimonious piece of journalism was that Harris was wrong, "militarily and morally" to have adopted area bombing and that he had been unduly harsh to the enemy, particluarly since the Germans had graceously limited the number of British citizens killed in the Blitz to only 60,000. The editorial went on to deplore the bombing of Dresden on the night of 13 February, 1945, because it was a town of ceramics, not arms and, according to the leader writer, by then the war was won. In quoting a figure of 60,000 people killed in Britain, the newspaper forgot to mention the six million of their own and other citizens killed by the Germans, or that the regime had ambitions to 'liquidate' (the expression in vogue by the Nazis at the time) many millions more. Furthermore, the war was anything but won by early 1945; the superb, if hard pressed, German Army was still a powerful, well equipped force although, thanks to Bomber Command, it was running out of fuel and supplies.

By the time of the raid Dresden had assumed a rather different role within the Fatherland. It was no longer confined to manufacturing artistic china figures. It was, in fact, full of German troops and munitions and a vital communications centre for the Eastern Front. It is primarily because of Don Bennett and his Pathfinders that Bomber Command became the major factor in determining the course of the war.

Otherwise intelligent people have, from time-to-time, felt moved to write off the significance of Bomber Command in the

1939-1945 war. Some have even claimed that Harris's campaign against Germany was a failure and a waste of Britain's resources. Such claims are an affront to the memory of more than 55,000 Bomber Command aircrew who gave their lives so that such ill-informed commentators could remain free to spread their distorted views. The facts are in print for all to inspect. They are supported by official records in Germany and Britain and the irrefutable picture that emerges is one of a mere 7 per cent of Britain's total service manpower, often prevented from acting to best advantage by higher authority, destroying the mighty Nazi war industry from the air and making it possible for citizen soldiers from Britain and America to take on and beat the most professional and powerful army in the history of warfare. Bomber Command did all that, saving the lives of many Allied soldiers. It was 'Bomber' Harris who saw it through but without Don Bennett the bombing offensive would have failed. He has sometimes been called 'The point of the spear'. He was certainly that during the war.

In their different ways each of Harris's group commanders gave of their best. But Don Bennett's contribution to Allied victory was on a different level. He brought to the task an expertise and intellect that revolutionised RAF thinking and certainly paved the way for victory in Europe. Many people, including some of his non-admirers, feel that Bennett should have been knighted for his masterly leadership of Pathfinder Force; there must be many who have done a great deal less for their country but who may nevertheless add the title 'Sir' before their name.

Don Bennett has been described as a religious non-churchgoer. He certainly believes in the existence of telepathy to the extent that when one of his Atlantic Ferry pilots went missing he immediately telephoned the man's wife and asked if she thought her husband was still alive because on several previous occasions he had known wives who were able to say with some conviction 'I know my husband is alive.' In this case he set up a search, the missing aircraft was found and they rescued the pilot off a frozen lake with the aid of two men and a dog sledge.

It is tempting to ask why Don Bennett ever left the RAF at the end of the war. He had reached Air rank, his unique expertise would have been valued and Ly Bennett enjoyed the life. However he had already promised to run British South American Airways and, if he had any doubts at the time, breaking his word would have been totally out of character.

He feels that Britain should have at least ten broadcasting companies, not just BBC and ITV as at present. Only by having a number of independent bodies can all views and opinions be given a fair hearing. He sees dangers in the media, newspapers or television, being too narrow.

During the war a head and shoulders photograph was taken of Don Bennett in his Air Vice-Marshal's uniform. That picture has probably done much to create a wrong impression of the man. In it he scowls with disapproval, rather like a housemaster about to admonish his pupils. Then when he stands up in front of people some of his natural reserve comes through as he delivers the words and this gives an impression that he is lacking in humour. Adept at small talk he is not; stand-up comic and teller of funny stories is outside his list of talents. But he is not slow with words of wit on the spur of the moment. For example, during the last interview for this book the Bennetts were looking after daughter Noreen's Alsatian, a young, rather undisciplined dog about the size of a small horse. Doggie was missing mistress and from outside the door came a prolonged howl, loud enough to drown all conversation. When it had finished Bennett said "I wonder who *he* is talking to?"

Today Don Bennett is in his mid seventies, active, alert as ever and still flying. His wife Ly, who plays a formidable game of tennis, remains a beautiful woman. Family photograph albums contain many pictures of the Bennetts skiing with their children, with their dogs, in various cars on the Monte Carlo Rally and the usual family snaps of holidays and parties for this or that occasion.

When he is not in England or Monte Carlo Don Bennett attends various functions abroad; the aircrew re-union in Canada, similar functions in Australia, New Zealand and so forth. He is President of the Pathfinder Association, President of the Aircrew Association and engaged in the task of bringing some cohesion to a number of separate Bomber Command associations. Although he has not been involved with large aircraft for many years his instant grasp of the latest developments in electronics, modern instrument presentations and, of course, state-of-the-art navigation techniques, is positively staggering. His ability to recall names, recent, from the past, within aviation, in the world of commerce or politics, is remarkable.

Although a strong claim could be made that his most outstanding achievement was the development and leadership of

Pathfinder Force any one of his other attainments would have marked him out as a man of distinction. His long distance seaplane flights in Mercury added valuable knowledge to the world of aviation. The Atlantic Ferry, formed on his recommendation against counter advice from the establishment, proved that the Atlantic could be flown, even during winter. His list of aeronautical qualifications in 1939 have probably never been equalled before or since. And he has tried to uphold the dignity and interests of his adopted country.

Throughout his eventful and remarkable life Don Bennett has been fortunate in enjoying the loyal support of a beautiful and intelligent wife. The role of 'woman behind the great man' is never an easy one, particularly when the personality concerned is a strong character with an outstanding brilliant mind. Although one could never induce Ly Bennett to talk about her less tranquil moments one suspects that she has suffered more than husband Donald when, from time to time, events have turned against him.

Air Vice-Marshal Donald Clifford Tyndall Bennett, CB., CBE., DSO., FRAeS., engineer, navigator supreme, political reformer, supporter of just causes, leader of men in peace and war — but above all else, Master Airman.

Index